Ordered By Words

Language
and Narration
in the
Novels of
William
Faulkner

Judith Lockyer

Southern Illinois
University Press

Carbondale and Edwardsville

Printed in the United States of America

Edited by Rebecca Spears Schwartz

Designed by David Ford

Production supervised by Natalia Nadraga

94 93 92 91   4 3 2 1

Library of Congress Cataloging-in-Publication Data

Lockyer, Judith.
   Ordered by words : language and narration in the novels of William
Faulkner / Judith Lockyer.
      p.   cm.
   Includes bibliographical references and index.
   1. Faulkner, William, 1897–1962—Technique.   2. Narration
(Rhetoric) I. Title.
   PS3511.A86Z879   1991
   813′.52—dc20
   ISBN 0-8093-1702-8   90-39482
                                                            CIP
                                                            Rev.

The paper used in this publication meets the minimum requirements of
American National Standard for Information Sciences—Permanance of Paper
for Printed Library Materials, ANSI Z39.48-1984. ∞

To Charles and Ruth Lockyer
and Nan

Contents

Preface

My title comes from Faulkner. In *Flags in the Dust*, Horace
Benbow describes himself as "ordered by words." Nearly a throw-
away line, the phrase names the idea about language that particularly intrigued this novelist who convinces a great many readers
that he has no easy relation to his medium. Deliberately ambiguous, the phrase suggests that words have power beyond their
capacity to organize reality; they might also direct behavior. And
Horace suggests that the power to do both of these things resides
outside himself. The phrase stayed with me as I began this project
to understand why there is so much in Faulkner's fiction that
worries over, even warns against itself. A great deal of Faulkner's
commentary about the act of writing—both inside and outside the
novels—centers on his desire to say everything about himself and
the world. That ambition suggests a desire for power that I think
Faulkner continually complicated. The most significant complication for me is his creation of the character who is ordered, even
haunted by words. Horace Benbow is the first fully drawn character whose life is shaped by his obsession with language, but he
is not the last. The issues change as Faulkner discovers new
complexities, but Horace's words echo in the characterizations
of Quentin Compson, Darl Bundren, Isaac McCaslin, and Gavin
Stevens. In these "men of words," I think Faulkner locates his
own anxieties about the possibilities and limitations in language.
The questions they raise about language also challenge Faulkner's
authority as writer. In that sense, their fates are also his. At the
very least, their stories reveal the intricacies of Faulkner's career-
long exploration of what language can and cannot achieve.

To follow this exploration, I have studied each character alone and in the contexts of the novels in which he appears. Because I am also claiming that the characters embody aspects of a conflict Faulkner himself experienced, I have relied on his commentary, again inside and outside of the fiction, about the issues the characters raise. My naming the characters "men of words" is deliberately gender specific to underscore Faulkner's own identification with the characters and his assumption that intellection is a masculine proclivity. In chapter 1, I discuss Horace Benbow's intensely personal struggle with language as it raises issues of identity and control that are also central to Faulkner as a writer just discovering his own voice. For example, Horace's affinity for the peaceful fixedness of poetry contributes to his own ineffectualness. At the same time, Horace provides Faulkner the means to distance himself from the allure of poetry and the absolute word (an allure Faulkner admits is powerful) without rejecting that power completely. Locating in Horace the desire for the absolute word of a poet allows Faulkner to explore, however tentatively, the idea that the novel allows him another power because of its stronger connection to the world, its openness to voices that can contradict or revise but also can reaffirm and always inform one another. In both *Flags in the Dust* and *Sanctuary*, Horace's presence warns against the desire for an absolute language, but still the voice of the other is present only as a halting interruption in the otherwise closed narrations of an idealized, mourned past.

Not until Faulkner creates Quentin Compson and Darl Bundren does he find the power in genuine exchange. Both characters are arguably mad, driven so by their desire to construct and order an immutable reality in language, but they appear in novels that find their strength in challenging the idea of a closed narration. In *The Sound and the Fury, Absalom, Absalom!*, and *As I Lay Dying*, as well as in *Light in August*, Faulkner disarms the threat of the multivoiced world by embracing it. In these novels, Faulkner makes the act of narration a metaphor for living in the world. Listening to other voices, articulating one's own, and integrating them all into an open-ended yet coherent whole are the major preoccupations of these novels. History, particularly America's legacy of racial strife, comes alive in characters whose voices together underscore the dialogic nature of narration. Meaning is given and taken away, but it never solidifies. The characters who yearn for the absolute word end up as emotional wrecks, in the state asylum, or dead. Their desire isolates them from the world's central truth—that language is a social construct. Furthermore, Mikhail Bakhtin's suggestion that meaning is situational helps explain the danger Faulkner finds in the obsession with absolutes. To deny that language derives its meaning from a context that brings together a socially constituted idea and an individual perception is to reject life. Yet Faulkner takes seriously Quentin's desire to shut himself away from the world that threatens his need for silence and permanence. In fact, the Quentin-like attraction to the absolute word frames the dialogue about language and narration that forms the subtext of all four novels.

According to Bakhtin, the absolute word, or authoritative discourse, comes to us from outside and can exert great power over us. Like the Sacred Writ, it is meant to be obeyed, not answered. We can choose to disobey, but we cannot alter the words themselves. Faulkner's men of words aspire to the power that absolute language holds, and in his later novels, Faulkner himself begins to succumb to it. The pattern of creating a dialogue about language remains, but the emphasis shifts. The questions he poses about writing, language, and reading are never rhetorical, although he knows well the power of a good rhetorical flourish. But to follow what Faulkner called "the course of it" is to engage questions about the application and revision of particular ideas, and it is significant that the novels Faulkner wrote in the last fifteen years of his life are generally less powerful than his earlier work. The reasons for that originate in the writing of *Go Down, Moses*. When he creates Ike McCaslin, Faulkner makes the struggle for authority also a struggle for an issue beyond individual control. Ike wants to transcend his family's legacy of racial fear and hate. He appears in a novel that echoes biblical language and purpose, that places Ike's mission in the larger context of America's anguish over racism. At the novel's close, Ike is alone in the cold recognition that his vow to relinquish his birthright has changed nothing, and part of Faulkner's open-ended, contentious approach to language disappears as well. While Ike may fail, his aspirations to find the absolute word and deed are empowered to a greater extent than are the similar desires of Horace or Quentin before him. Faulkner's change in direction is subtle, but it offers a new way to read *Go Down, Moses* and the novels which follow it.

Finally, I discuss the new prominence of the character Gavin Stevens, whose project to translate the Old Testament into the purity of its original language signifies Faulkner's own efforts to render his personal truth into a public one. The efforts make Faulkner less open to the prospect of outside influence and more inclined toward authoritative discourse. Concerned about the state of the world and increasingly aware of himself as a public figure, Faulkner becomes less questioning and more didactic. Although Gavin Stevens is never presented as an unqualified authority, his presence grows increasingly respectable after *Go Down, Moses*. And his aspirations to find the absolute word do not fail like Ike's do. In fact, they echo in the language and design of all of Faulkner's books beginning with *Intruder in the Dust* (1948). Faulkner's sense of his own moral responsibility to warn against human folly requires that he close off a part of his work to the answering voice. He does not abandon the dialogue he began thirty years before in *Flags in the Dust*, but his efforts to assert his own authority certainly alter it. Although by most accounts, his late work is not his best, Faulkner's increasingly apparent desire for authority complicates the connections between the individual and the world, between language and its context, that he has been exploring from the beginning. Faulkner's insistence that life is narrative, based on the preeminence of language in our lives, never wavers.

To trace the development of his ideas about language is to act on the impulse to order that Faulkner understood so well. It is knowing the allure of ordering—both to arrange comprehensibly and to command or direct—that pushes Faulkner beyond any simple assumption of what it means to speak, to read, and above all, to write.

To write about Faulkner is truly to enter a conversation that shows no signs of losing vigor. For my part in the conversation,

I am indebted to Joseph Blotner, Gary Stonum, Karl Zender, and James Watson, whose work in Faulkner's life and letters illuminated the novels for me. I have also learned a great deal from the critical insights that John Irwin, André Bleikasten, John Matthews, and Myra Jehlen have brought to the study of Faulkner's language. For his generous support of this project from start to finish, I give very special thanks to Joseph Blotner. I am also indebted to Robert Weisbuch for his attention to my manuscript and to my colleagues Charles Crupi, James Diedrick, and Catherine Lamb for their interest in discussing my ideas. All provided me with much appreciated responses and questions that helped to shape my thinking. And finally, for her excellent typing of its many versions, I thank Susan Richmond.

Ordered by Words

1

Horace Benbow and Faulkner's Troubled Authority

"Perhaps that's what makes one a poet . . . being able to sustain a fine obliviousness of the world and its compulsions."

"A book is a writer's secret life, the dark twin of a man: you can't reconcile them."—Julius Kauffman in *Mosquitoes*

In *Sartoris* (1929), William Faulkner's third published novel, Horace Benbow writes to his sister Narcissa, "I have always been ordered by words," and in doing so he articulates a habit of mind that Faulkner would explore and worry over for more than thirty years.[1] Horace's sentence explicitly recognizes that language can both define and command; its passive construction implicitly questions the ownership of that power. While he is not the first Faulknerian character to be dominated by his anxieties over the inefficacy of language, Horace is the first to embody both disbelief and faith in language. In his second novel, *Mosquitoes* (1927), Faulkner stages a series of debates about the efficacy of language. Far less sophisticated than his later dialogic approach, the sparring between Dawson Fairchild, the word's anxious advocate, and Julius Kauffman, Fairchild's self-appointed critic, sets the stage for Faulkner's career-long exploration of the writer's power. Some of the issues they raise, such as the disjunction between words and

1

their referents, and between words and action, are delineated much more fully in Horace Benbow's tortured self-awareness. Horace believes in the power and truth of words. He is a bookish romantic who lives within a system he has constructed out of words, and his words often trap him in thought-filled inaction. He also knows that his belief in language's power to create order and meaning can isolate him from the imperfect, unstable, and often uncontrollable world, and that knowledge is both the source of his anguish and the impetus for his life. A self-described "failed poet," Faulkner knew well the pain and pleasure of the consciousness circumscribed by an idea of language. In the 1956 *Paris Review* interview, Faulkner spoke of the writer's "splendid failure to do the impossible . . . [to match] the work to the image."[2] And in the same interview, Faulkner also commented on a crucial distinction in his mind between the poet and the novelist—the poet has a greater power to distill and preserve experience. A year later, Faulkner clarified the poet's power by defining poetry as "some moving, passionate moment of the human condition distilled to its absolute essence."[3] For Faulkner, poetry was the higher art because of its greater precision, its higher power to name exactly and thus *be* the essence of human experience. His own "failure" to achieve this power informs all of his writing life, for his imagination would not dismiss easily the person who is ordered by words. Horace Benbow is the most simply drawn of a character that Faulkner would rename and rewrite again and again.

As Joseph Blotner carefully delineates, Faulkner created in Horace Benbow a character whose affinity for poetry mirrored his own.[4] Faulkner's connection to the numerous failed poets in his novels is tantalizingly real and, of course, never absolute. The often-noted fact that Faulkner's fiction actively challenges the boundaries separating life from art, any one of his texts from another, as well as his words from other writers', provides an opening into the ongoing critical discussion of those connections.

In 1929 Faulkner published a second novel, *The Sound and the Fury*, which introduced an infinitely more complex variation of Horace in Quentin Compson. Twenty-six years later, Faulkner would remark to Jean Stein that "Ishmael is the witness in *Moby Dick* as I am Quentin in *The Sound and the Fury*" (Blotner, *Faulkner*, 2: 1522).[5] While it is rare that Faulkner made such connections explicit, the persistence of characters who are ordered by words testifies to the power of their presence in his imagination. Faulkner returned to Horace in *Sanctuary* (1931) and to Quentin in *Absalom, Absalom!* (1936). We know as well that the Quentin Compson of "A Justice," "Lion," and the first published version of "The Old People" literally evolves into the Ike McCaslin of *Go Down, Moses* (1940).[6] Textual evidence also supports the evolution of Horace into Gavin Stevens, whose preoccupation with words is woven into the narratives of six novels.[7] About the same time that he was writing Horace, Faulkner's fascination with the "man of words" also led him to explore the unstable limits of narrative power in Darl Bundren's demise in *As I Lay Dying* (1930). The period between 1927 and 1931 was intensely productive for Faulkner, and connections abound among *Flags in the Dust, Sartoris* (the truncated version of *Flags in the Dust*), *The Sound and the Fury*, the two versions of *Sanctuary*, and *As I Lay Dying*. Horace Benbow shares more than a troubled idealism with Quentin, Darl, Ike, and Gavin. All five characters are bound by an intense, complex relation to words that often intersects with that of the writer's. Each one is tormented by his desire to do the impossible—to create, order, and preserve the essence of experience in words. And each lives with the sense that he, too, is a kind of failed poet. To discover the genesis of that failure, Faulkner begins to challenge the limitations of the language that makes any meaning possible.

For him, the word's greatest limitation was its inability to recover the thing it names. Faulkner's novels always unfold in the recognition of the potential for loss in the world. Language and the act of writing are so bound to the idea of loss—of the word's referent, the writer's self, even of time itself—that to write fiction was, for Faulkner, always to contend with its presence. In his 1931 essay on the writing of *Sartoris*, Faulkner makes clear that loss was an inextricable part of writing for him from the beginning:

4 · Ordered by Words

All that I really desired was a touchstone simply; a simple word or gesture, having known twice before the agony of ink, nothing served but that I try [*to evoke*] by main strength to recreate between the covers of a book the world as I was already preparing to lose and regret.[8]

As I will show, the language of that novel does work to preserve a life fast disappearing. Novel writing, then, allowed Faulkner to confront the terrible element of imprecision in language, the limits of its authority, and to put that up against his belief in the power of the word to assert the self and to constitute order and meaning in the world.

Faulkner's ideas about language and narration have, of course, intrigued scholars from the beginning, and the more recent, burgeoning arena of literary theory has given new life to Faulkner studies. Faulkner's sensitivity to the presence of loss in language invites a deconstructionist's reading, and among the most provocative is John T. Matthews' book, *The Play of Faulkner's Language*, which links Faulkner's understanding of the danger in writing, the mistaken belief that the word can recover experience, to what Jacques Derrida calls the supplemental nature of language.[9] Matthews' argument, that Faulkner's sophisticated understanding of the dangers of language keeps the idea of meaningful play alive in his fiction, opens the language of Faulkner to fruitful scrutiny. Earlier critics, like Walter Slatoff in *Quest for Failure*, noted the tension in the novels but read it as Faulkner's attempt (often unsuccessful) to resolve his idea of language as the complete revelation of truth.[10] But Matthews overlooks Faulkner's deep awareness of language as a social entity, as a construct as inextricable from time and place as his characters. And for all it adds to our comprehension of Faulkner's narratives, deconstructionism finally leaves unexplained the persistent desire for authority present in Faulkner's language. John Irwin speaks to Faulkner's struggle with authority in *Doubling and Incest/Repetition and Revenge*. His reading of Quentin Compson's struggle to achieve authority as it mirrors Faulkner's compulsion to assert authority by authoring opens the discussion of threatened power in Faulkner's relation to language.[11] Although his analysis is generally limited to *The Sound*

and the Fury and *Absalom, Absalom!*, Irwin makes a central
point when he notes that there is more than a little of Quentin
Compson in Faulkner. Both seem "fated to retell in different
ways the same story again and again," and both experience those
retellings in part as failures.[12] The story that Faulkner retells and
revises with each of the five characters is that of the doomed man
of words who struggles for peace in a world threatened by the
past, a present that doesn't quite fit, and the spectre of the character's own helplessness.

Beginning with Horace Benbow in *Flags in the Dust*, the dialogue between Faulkner's man of words and the novels that give
him life allows the author to create and revise his understanding
of our relation to language. Through these characters, and in the
novels in which they appear, Faulkner deliberately creates tension
between the ideas of the loss and attainment of power in language.
That tension in turn creates a dialogue that he weaves into the
text of his novels. The word *dialogue* now conjures the name
Mikhail Bakhtin, and it is his theory of the novel as discourse that
informs many of my readings of Faulkner's novels. Bakhtin's idea
of the word as positioned between its referent and human consciousness, as being both a part of a social construct and created
by its user, illuminates Faulkner's idea of language as both loss
and power.[13] If language exists prior to any given user and in a
specific social and historical context, then its meaning must reside,
in part, outside the user as well. The presence of the other, the
part of language not in its user's control, threatens the power that
Faulkner's men of words desire. In "Discourse in the Novel,"
Bakhtin begins by distinguishing between the language of poetry
and that of the novel. He calls poetry a "single-languaged genre"
that reflects a unity of style and perspective that necessarily closes
it off from other voices or contexts that would alter it.[14] The ideal
poetic language is "monological," like "authoritative discourse,"
and remains above interaction with any other language; its meaning is closed off from any context other than the poet's own.
Authoritative discourse, such as the Bible or political polemic,
derives its power from asserting claimed truth; so too poetry
remains beyond the answering voice. Bakhtin defines the condi-

tions of most poetic genres as following the spirit of Saussure's idea of stylistic unity, which presupposes both "a unity of language (in the sense of a system of general normative forms) and on the other hand the unity of an individual person realizing himself in this language" ("Discourse in the Novel," 264). Although a part of Faulkner always regrets never having achieved that "single language," his decision to write novels recognizes the word's inextricable ties to social, historical, and personal contexts. Because Bakhtin's work on the novel centers on a similar idea of language, it provides me a particularly useful theoretical framework. My interest is not to develop a detailed correlation between the complexities of Bakhtin's theories and Faulkner's novels; rather, I want to point to the general principles of *The Dialogic Imagination* as they provide context for my readings of Faulkner's novels. To broaden my use of the word *dialogue*, I draw on Bakhtin's definition of *dialogism* as the notion that the word must compete with shifting meanings for the things it seeks to name. Bakhtin defines the novel as the genre most often formed by dialogical discourse, by the languages of various voices that compete with and influence one another. But the dialogue in Faulkner's novels is also often a complicated debate between two opposite ideas of language. It is not Faulkner's unequivocal belief that "the word in language is half someone else's" ("Discourse in the Novel," 293) but rather his continual challenge to that belief—even in the novels that so clearly celebrate it—that creates the dialogue I am concerned with.

Faulkner's recognition of the other in language was most uncomfortable when he represented people most obviously different from him—women, blacks, and those who are both. Faulkner once commented that creating female characters was for him a difficult pleasure because "I know very little about them."[15] And the novels themselves reveal a perspective that is predominantly Southern, white, and male. I make that point in the assumption that language and ideology are inextricable; to clarify, I turn again to Bakhtin. In a provocative essay that turns Bakhtin's idea of novelistic discourse back on Bakhtin, Wayne Booth investigates the inescapable bias of any discourse, but particularly of literary interpretation, since we all "speak with our ideology."[16] The definition of ideology here corresponds to Bakhtin's use of the term as more basic than a particular political stance; simply, it names any social system. Language is therefore ideologic because it is a social construct. Bakhtin perceives ideology as inherent in not just the speech of characters but in the language that represents their environments, thoughts, and actions: "The activity of a character in a novel is always ideologically demarcated: he lives and acts in an ideological world *of his own*" ("Discourse in the Novel," 355, italics mine). If every character in a novel speaks and acts out of a particular ideological context, it follows that every novelist does as well. The work of feminist critics and the New Historicists turns on this idea, and my readings of Faulkner's novels are informed by the growing body of criticism that connects Faulkner's women and blacks to the context in which he wrote them.[17] To say that Faulkner's women and blacks reflect our culture's patriarchal definitions of both groups is true and yet too simple. While it will be important to my argument at times to discuss Faulkner's connections to a racist and sexist culture, more significant is that fact that his blacks and women always appear as the other, as different from white men, whether for bad or for good. Faulkner's acute sense of the difference in women and blacks has significant consequences for his sense of the other in language. Early in his career, and particularly in *Flags in the Dust* and *Sanctuary*, the difference is primarily a threat. As I hope to make clear, my interest is not in ferreting out evidence of Faulkner's racism or sexism but in showing how Faulkner's struggle with his authorial powers are played out in his language. Precisely because of Faulkner's difference from and interest in blacks and women, the issues of race and gender—as they are defined in his texts—offer significant insights into his relation to language.

One of the most alluring and persistent contradictions in our culture is the idea that unity or universality and individuality are equally valuable and simultaneously possible. Faulkner's increasing interest in universalizing the particular and his abiding valuation of the seif are absolutely connected to his uneasy belief that language is both a social and a personal tool. His familiar description of the onset of his most productive writing reveals a variation of the two antithetical ideas side by side:

> Beginning with *Sartoris* I discovered that my own little postage stamp of native soil was worth writing about . . . . It opened up a gold mine of other peoples, so I created a cosmos of my own. I can move these people around like God, not only in space but in time too. (Meriwether and Millgate, eds., *Lion in the Garden*, 255)

First he pays tribute to the richness of his "native soil," acknowledging the part that the South's history and people have in his fiction. Faulkner's sense of the world inside his novels and its connection to language comes out of what Bakhtin would call his recognition of the "heteroglossia" in novelistic language. In "Discourse in the Novel," Bakhtin says that heteroglossia, or the social and historical presence in all spoken language, becomes the language of the other always present in the novelist's words (263). Faulkner's discovery in writing *Flags in the Dust/Sartoris* is in part, then, the discovery that his words are filled with life beyond his own power to define. That understanding gives a new richness to his work, but it also wars with an impulse toward absolute control that wants to deny the other.

Faulkner also observes that writing allowed him to create a world and to move his creations around "like God." His assertion is modified from the 1931 essay wherein he comments that his characters were "composed partly from what they were in actual life and partly from what they should have been and were not: thus I improved on (*nature*), God, who, dramatic though He be, has no sense, no feeling for, theatre" (Blotner, "William Faulkner's Essay," 123). The writer's will to be God, or even more than God, to wield absolute power, necessarily closes off interaction with another and separates text from context as the word struggles to become *the word*. The Bible, or any sacred text, contains the authoritative discourse that Bakhtin says "permits no play with the context framing it" ("Discourse in the Novel," 343). Embedded in the word *authority* is the word *author*, and embedded in Faulkner's writing is the dialogue that makes this relationship an issue. To be "like God" is of course not the same as being God. Faulkner knows that very well, and his knowledge is both a torment and the source of another power that he begins to define in *Sartoris*. For Horace Benbow, being ordered by words means both to structure experience comprehensibly by putting it into words and to effect action with language. Faulkner describes writing *Sartoris* with the same desire to arrange and to control through language that confines Horace's life. But Faulkner denies Horace the power that he celebrates and instead centers all of his doubts about that power in Horace's anxious person. Yet *Sartoris* was first *Flags in the Dust*, and Faulkner's struggle to get it published attests to the author's concrete connections to his character. His first reader, Horace Liveright, found the novel rambling and filled with too much language and too little plot. So did the next eleven publishers. To get the book published, Faulkner finally and reluctantly agreed to Ben Wasson's more ruthless editing that drastically cut the story of Horace Benbow. But the original, more lengthy development of the Horace Benbow story in both *Flags* and the first version of *Sanctuary*, written shortly afterward, reveal Horace to be a far more central concern of Faulkner's than the more familiar texts allow.[18] The Horace Benbow of *Sartoris* and of the 1931 *Sanctuary* is not drastically different from the Horace of the original drafts, but his later characterization lacks the more substantive motivation of the earlier drafts, which centers on his obsession with the dangers of female sexuality and on his sense of failure to cope with either his inner life or outside circumstances. Noel Polk's essay on the two versions of *Sanctuary* gives a particularly helpful perspective on Horace.[19] Polk argues that the edited material reveals more fully Horace's nightmarish childhood fantasies, thus connecting his present obsessive fears about women and sexuality to a half-perceived Oedipal trauma. Gracefully avoiding a definitively Freudian interpretation, Polk suggests connections between Horace and the traumas suffered by Temple Drake and Popeye, as well as to the sexual dread that haunts Quentin Compson, thus providing convincing evidence that Horace's psychological entrapment informs much of Faulkner's work between 1927 and 1931. I will argue that the connections between Horace's problems with female sexuality and his obsession with the dangers

in language tell us a great deal about the unresolved anxieties
about language that mark the flowering of Faulkner's writing
life. The sense of failure that haunts Horace in both *Flags* and
Sanctuary implicates language and, by extension, stands in implicit challenge to Faulkner's role as writer. In Horace, Faulkner
explores the limitations of his power as author and comes perhaps
too close to perceiving his own deeply personal ties to the act of
writing. Horace's struggle with language is intensely personal; in
both *Flags* and *Sanctuary* it is closely connected to Faulkner's
fears about sex and death. In the 1931 essay, Faulkner says that
Flags was his speculation "on time and death" (124). We know too
that during this time Faulkner was falling in love with Estelle
Oldham Franklin. James Watson's excellent study of the connections between Faulkner's letters and his fiction reveals several
instances in which the language that describes Estelle is identical
to the language that describes Narcissa and the manuscript itself.[20]
Although I am not the first to suggest that Faulkner and Horace
share certain traits, I do not mean to say that Horace is Faulkner.
Rather, I believe that insofar as Horace's anxieties are tied to
issues of authorship, they can tell us much about Faulkner's own
relation to language. Horace's love for Narcissa, his tortured
thinking about Belle and Little Belle, his nausea on hearing Temple's story are all tied to his desire for the perfect, immutable vase.
And that desire is connected in Faulkner's imagination to the act
of writing.

From his introduction in *Flags*, Horace Benbow's "air of fine
and delicate futility" saturates his every appearance in the novel.[21]
He is an idealist of the dreamiest sort. That idealism separates
Horace from the world in which he must function, even from his
beloved sister:

> In the adjoining room Horace lay while that wild, fantastic futility
> of his voyaged in lonely regions of its own beyond the moon, about
> meadows nailed with firmamented stars to the ultimate roof of
> things, where unicorns filled the neighing air with galloping, or
> grazing or lay supine in golden-hoofed repose. (187)

The narrator's extravagant and yet precise language illustrates
Horace's own endeavor. Horace creates a world out of words.

Language gives him the power to shape and nail down his reality. But by escaping into an imaginary otherworld, Horace designs his own defeat. His search is for absolutes, but his pursuit boxes him into a kind of emotional absence. In addition to making him sound a bit silly, the narrator emphasizes that Horace's fantasies contribute to the general aura of ineffectiveness surrounding him. The connection between Horace's imaginings and the words that give them substance is strong, thus implicating language in the general failure of his life. We learn that Horace plans to resume his law practice because of his "love for printed words, for the dwelling-places of books" (184), which completely removes law from the realities of its practice. In *Sanctuary*, Horace argues with Lee Goodwin that his case has promise because he can ascribe "the law, justice, civilization" to Goodwin's defense, and we know how very abstract and absolute those words are to Horace.[22]

Lawyer Benbow, educated at Sewanee and Oxford, is the first of Faulkner's verbose intellectuals. In the characterizations of Horace, Gavin Stevens, and Quentin Compson lies an unmistakable jab at the negative effects of higher education. Horace's being a lawyer only strengthens the indictment against him. He depends upon words to know the world to a far greater degree than any other character in either *Flags* or *Sanctuary*. His profession also labels him as a man who relies heavily on written codes of conduct, who believes fervently in the universe that man's intellect—and Faulkner does identify intellect as masculine—has circumscribed. In *Sanctuary*, Horace's faith in justice and his legal defense of Lee Goodwin crumble, making all his words a sham. We are told from the outset that Horace's trust in language is misplaced. In *Flags*, Horace's talk is described in "staccato babbling" (180), and in *Sanctuary*, Ruby Lamar listens to his "quick, faintly outlandish voice, the voice of a man given to much talk and not much else" (14). In *Flags*, Horace Benbow is a timid young man who is "born aloft on his flaming verbal wings" (180); in *Sanctuary*, he has become a forty-three-year-old man, tortured by incestuous desires and disillusioned by his loveless marriage, clinging frantically to the last of his romantic illusions—that he can effect justice by talking. When Horace does speak, his words are usually fanciful and elaborately dramatic. The narrator clearly establishes a connection between Horace's effete romanticism and his penchant for words.

Horace's belief in the language of imagination augments his faith in the world of the law. Critics have often noted the appropriateness of Horace's glassblowing hobby in *Flags*. He speaks rapturously of a "small chaste shape in clear glass," of "preserved flowers [and the] sound of pipes crystallized" (179–80). We see that art is a means for Horace to realize and preserve his desire for harmony and permanent, unblemished beauty. The word *chaste* also conjures an association with female sexuality that informs Horace's artistic efforts and suggests another strand of the much-discussed Horace/Keats/Faulkner tangle. One only has to read a few of Faulkner's poems to see that he certainly held to the tradition of making the female the embodiment of poetic inspiration and its subject as well. For example, two lines from "Une Ballad des Femmes Perdues" suggest that female chastity vexed him early on: "They dance with quick feet on my lute strings / With the abandon of boarding school virgins."[23] Females lost, especially to sexual experience, haunt the imaginations of both Faulkner and Horace. Art seems to have been the only hope of preserving the ephemeral, perhaps illusory state of female innocence. The idea that art is immutable echoes Faulkner's belief in the higher power of poetry to create and protect experience.[24] Although centered in the neurosis of Horace Benbow, echoes of poets and poetry resound in *Flags*. Throughout the novel, allusions to both surround Horace; Faulkner both implicates poetry in Horace's failure and relies on it to elaborate Horace's character. His very name suggests an association with one of the first poets and thus a belief in the power of words to carry meaning and to influence others. The possibility of a connection, in the reader's mind, between the two Horaces indicates the narrator's faith in the evocative power of words. But given the impotence of Horace Benbow, any comparison must also consider him the rather enervated descendant of the Latin poet. Furthermore, the allusions to poetry generally work to undercut Horace's belief in words and to expose him as hopelessly idealistic.

The most negative reference is to Keats' "Ode on a Grecian Urn," which is of course both a Horatian ode and among the poems Faulkner most admired. The contradiction in damning Horace with this particular poem introduces the paradoxical relationship to poetry that Faulkner explores further in Gavin Stevens and Ike McCaslin. In the following passage, the allusion creates an explicit connection between poetry and Horace's glassblowing, and labels both as stultifyingly romantic:

> [He] produced one almost perfect vase of clear amber, larger, more richly and chastely serene, which he kept always on his night table and called by his sister's name in the intervals of apostrophizing both of them impartially in his moments of rhapsody over the realization of the meaning of peace and the unblemished attainment of it, as "Thou still unravished bride of quietude." (*Flags*, 190–91)

Critics often cite this passage as evidence of Horace's idealism and desire for stasis; I would add that Horace views poetry, his sister's name, and all language as the means to attain and hold on to his ideal of peace.[25] James Watson makes a significant connection between Horace's obsession and Faulkner's attraction to it by calling attention to a letter Faulkner wrote to his Aunt McLean in the spring of 1928. In it, Faulkner describes Estelle as "like a lovely vase" (Watson, *Letters and Fictions*, 67). And in describing the writing of *The Sound and the Fury*, which also took place at this time, Faulkner talks of never having had a sister and of making a vase for himself. Looking ahead to a time when words might fail him, he talks of knowing even then that he would not "live forever inside of it."[26] The vase/woman/book connections are clearly present in his imagination, but equally present is his knowledge that he must distance himself from his words. For all that he shares with Horace, Faulkner also writes to separate himself from the habit of mind that so threatened his character.

The distinction Faulkner makes between himself and Horace is clarified in looking at the connection between them. Horace's glassblowing is tied to his love of language: " 'The meaning of peace,' he said to himself again, releasing the grave words one by one within the cool bell of silence into which a dying fall pure as silver and crystal struck lightly together" (*Flags*, 184). His words are like shaped, struck glass, an association that the entire passage reinforces. In writing, Faulkner exercises the same kind of power through language as Horace does. Words shape experience, and they also promise to preserve it. Horace's words *create* the peace and purity he desires, even while they exist in the paradoxical "bell of silence." Horace's making of silence a sacrosanct entity introduces a notion that Faulkner will explore further in his other idealistic failures. Horace desires a silence into which only he can release language. In a nice twist to the paradox, the phrase "with a dying fall" echoes *The Tempest* and of course Eliot's "The Love Song of J. Alfred Prufrock." The allusion triggers an association between Horace and Prufrock, who serves as Faulkner's model of the self-conscious failure. Prufrock listens to "voices dying with a dying fall," and Horace listens to his own voice "linger with a dying fall."[27] The difference underscores Horace's personal failure, for even as he tries to arrive at peace, the movement of the entire novel works to undermine any hope for permanence or harmony as we see the disorienting effects of the twentieth century on Jefferson, Mississippi. That Faulkner talked of *Flags* as an effort to evoke a disappearing world connects him to Horace but also transcends him. Faulkner successfully completes his book and in doing so finds his own power. Also, the allusion to the poem enriches the passage. By deepening our understanding of Horace, it underscores the ability of language to evoke images with precision. Allusion draws attention to the evocative power of language, thus undercutting slightly the overt message that words are divorced from reality.

Horace's words, of course, do not match reality, the world in which he must live. They cushion him, for example, from the Narcissa we see. In *Flags*, she is not at all the "bride of quietude" Horace wants her to be. And certainly in *Sanctuary*, she is exposed as conniving and shallow and the person who profoundly shatters any hope Horace may still have held for peace. But Horace tries to make Narcissa the embodiment of purity by saying that she is. The articulation brings him comfort and peace, and it is this belief that words, particularly poems, create reality that defeats him.

Yet Horace himself indicts poetry as escapist and unconnected to reality: "The law, like poetry, is the final resort of the lame, the halt, the imbecile, and the blind. I dare say Caesar invented the law business to protect himself against poets" (*Flags*, 199). When the negative character himself makes comments about the institution he champions and the narrator scorns, he defuses some of the criticism aimed at him. Horace's self-disparagement introduces the notion that his facility with words grants him a worldly wisdom, which he delivers to the ignorant from an experienced distance. He has a jaded self-awareness that makes the reader wonder if Horace really considers himself a complete failure. Horace certainly recognizes the world's suspicions of poetry. He even realizes a disjunction between active participation in the world and the dreamy folly attributed to poets, but Horace never truly forsakes poetic language. Faulkner, the "failed poet," echoes Horace's ambivalence by having the frantic Byron Snopes engage Virgil Beard to transcribe his panting love letters to Narcissa. These present-day bards appear to carry the brunt of Faulkner's mockery, but the point of that witty renaming is blunted later when the narrator muses that "some Homer should sing the saga, of the mule and his place in the South" (313). The fact that this suggestion is followed by a long and beautifully evocative tribute to the mule is further evidence that Faulkner wrote *Flags* to commemorate a South he feared he was losing. For Faulkner, Horace Benbow appears to embody his own haunted affinity for the power of poetry.

Horace's close ties to language grant him a greater awareness of its place in his life, as well as the means to expound on its role in all our lives. Through him, Faulkner gives life to a significant part of his dialogue about the nature of language and of writing. Horace's self-awareness complicates his characterization (he is not a simple failure) and establishes a precedent for later Faulknerian intellectuals. At the end of *Flags*, we see the newly married Horace reminisce about his home in Jefferson and the sister he has idealized into the "unravished bride of quietude." Horace ultimately wants to use his words to create a pure and permanent silence, a desire Quentin Compson will magnify. To achieve his goal, Horace writes a letter to Narcissa and begins to come to terms with the marriage that he already fears may have been a mistake:

> The words he had just written echoed yet in his mind with a little gallant and whimsical sadness, and for the time being he had quitted the desk and the room and the town and all the crude and blatant newness . . . again that wild and fantastic futility of his roamed unchallenged. . . . The pen moved again.
>
> "Perhaps fortitude is a sorry imitation of something worthwhile. . . . But not to those who carry peace along with them as the candle-flame carries the light. I have always been ordered by words, but it seems that I can even restore assurance to my own cowardice by cozening it a little. I dare say you cannot read this, as usual, or reading it, it will not mean anything to you. But you will have served your purpose anyway, thou still unravished bride of quietude." (397–98)

First we see that writing allows Horace to escape the hard reality of his new life in Kinston. He sustains his nostalgia for home through the artful arrangement of words, and we sense that expressing his feelings engages Horace as much as the feelings themselves. As he continues, his subject becomes his writing the letter.[28] His words smack of self-indulgence, but they also reveal an interesting ambivalence toward the act of writing.

Horace acknowledges, albeit in language that may escape the pragmatic Narcissa, that her response to this communication is of little importance. In fact, letters are the best means of communication for Horace because they allow him to create and even preserve thought and silence. Narcissa is his "bride of quietude," an appropriate muse. He does not want her to reply, for breaking the silence would admit imperfection, which here is synonymous with dialogue. Again, self-expression takes precedence over communication. Horace closes the act of letter writing by denying the reader's contribution. The fact that Narcissa will be the most passive of readers enables Horace to write; he fills her silence with his words. He knows that he writes to "order" himself, and he believes in the power of his words to bring him the peace he wants.

At the same time, he calls the act of writing a trick. As he finishes the letter, Horace thinks that "though one can lie about others with ready and extemporaneous promptitude, to lie about oneself requires deliberation and a careful choice of expression" (399). Horace seems perfectly content with the idea that he is lying; his words imply a distinction between lying *about* himself and *to* himself. But the distinction grows less clear when we recall that Narcissa's response to his words is less important than his own. Earlier in *Flags*, Horace tells Narcissa that "lying is a struggle for survival . . . little puny man's way of dragging circumstances to fit his preconception of himself as a figure in the world" (222). Horace's observation universalizes and even distinguishes lying as a life-or-death issue. Insofar as the novelist drags circumstances around to fit an idea of the world, fiction is a form of lying, and of self-assertion, which is of course still a "puny" effort. To lie or to trick implies a deviousness that Horace intends but also makes noble.

Horace Benbow is not the only person who rearranges circumstance with language, and he is not the only person who writes letters. Byron Snopes' letters to Narcissa are also a vain effort to realize his desire for her. John Matthews' discussion of the Byron-Virgil episodes makes clear the ways in which Faulkner explores writing as representation and deferment; Byron's letters are full of yearning for Narcissa, whose actual presence they can never create. The letters establish no connection between writer and reader, but Horace's relation to language complicates Faulkner's recognition of the supplemental nature of language with an equally strong recognition of language as self-authorizing.[29] The belief that saying something makes it so and the knowledge that people lie combine in the unsettling conclusion that language, imperfect as it is, is our only means to truth. It often even *becomes* the truth. How to make that happen develops into the important issue for Faulkner the writer. Myra Jehlen makes a central point about the much-discussed Faulknerian idea of truth when she notes that his primary anxiety is not that truth is subjective but that we are ill-equipped to perceive it as it exists. Faulkner's great respect for the power of individual perspective is evident in all his most critically acclaimed novels; the narrative strategies of *The Sound and the Fury*, *As I Lay Dying*, and *Absalom, Absalom!* are built on that power. At the same time, the fiction is replete with references to universal human truths and continually strives to articulate them. Reconciling what can be seen as private and public ideas of language requires a definition of all language as a social entity. I argue that Faulkner both knows that and wants to forget it. Faulkner's belief in universals, his faith in public or commonly shared language is common knowledge, but as Jehlen and later André Bleikasten have helped us to realize, truth for Faulkner is inextricably connected to the white Southern culture in which he lived.[30] The extent to which Faulkner knew this is impossible to determine, but his fiction is full of the tensions between the universal and the individual, or for my purposes, between absolute and dialogic language. To return to Horace, the trick of words makes him brave; language effects the desired change. Thus Horace deliberates more carefully when he lies about himself—the act carries more significance because it is more subjective than other subjective acts. Horace is more comfortable with this paradox than with the unpredictable, often corrupt world of human action.

For Horace Benbow, the subjectivity of language *is* reality or truth. For Faulkner, Horace's idea of language is true but as flawed as he is. Although Horace's failures are linked to his love of words, it is also the source of his power. Horace's skill with language allows him to interpret the life he sees around him. His affinity for words gives him a greater aptitude for making meaning, which also becomes the life's work of Quentin and Darl and Gavin and Ike. Often his language is precise and accurate. The opening pages of *Sanctuary* pit Horace, who carries a book, against Popeye, who thinks it is a pistol. Horace hears a bird, whose sound is "meaningless and profound" (4). The oxymoron enriches this introductory, apparently chance meeting of the two antithetical characters, whom many critics consider equally negative.[31] Through the indirection of trope, the narrator sets up the tension: the words are significant and insignificant. Popeye takes no note of the bird; Horace tries to recall the local name for it, to place it.

One of Horace's first observations about Popeye illustrates his facility with language: "He smells black . . . he smells like black stuff that ran out of Bovary's mouth and down upon her bridal veil when they raised her head" (7). The analogy he makes between Popeye and Emma Bovary characterizes Horace as literary; it allows him to order the situation. Later Popeye derisively calls him "the professor" (9), and the narrator of *Sanctuary* sustains the image of Horace as an ineffective intellectual. But the analogy primarily and vividly associates Popeye with poison and death, an observation that demonstrates the sensitivity and accuracy of Horace's literary mind. By revealing Horace's familiarity with Flaubert, the narrator qualifies the failure of this innocent idealist. Horace has obviously read Flaubert's account of the misguided and dangerous female in pursuit of sexual and romantic fulfillment, something with which *he* is identified. Yet Horace is the character who first connects the evil to Popeye, who is portrayed as relentlessly unromantic, nonverbal, and machinelike. Horace's acquaintance with language has made him both a hopeless dreamer and an acute observer. Horace reaches into literature to name accurately Popeye's destructive nature and thus prefigures the central action of the novel, which Faulkner never actually tells. Instead we discover, by piecing together what the narrator and characters tell us, that Popeye has raped Temple Drake with a corn cob; Horace's delayed horror of Popeye's evil is also Faulkner's.[32] They also share the other horror—of female sexuality—and that complicates Faulkner's control over Horace's failed life. André Bleikasten's essay on Emma Bovary and Temple Drake as incarnations of the mythic hysterical woman offers a strong argument for what *Sanctuary* reveals about Horace's and Faulkner's revulsion at Temple Drake.[33] I would add that the culture-bound ideas about women that permeate *Sanctuary* reveal themselves in the very language that appears to include the female but cannot quite do so.

Just as Horace stands as Faulkner's acknowledgment of his own desire to protect experience in words, Horace himself admits that his love of language has helped to make him hopelessly unfit to meet the world's standards for a young man. He is full of ardent desires that remain too long unacted upon. His middle-aged life does not match his youthful dreams, as we learn in *Sanctuary* when he explains why he plans to leave his wife, Belle:

> It's because the package drips. All the way home it drips and drips, until after a while I follow myself to the station and stand aside and watch Horace Benbow take that box off the train and start home

with it, changing hands every hundred steps, and I followed him, thinking Here lies Horace Benbow in a fading series of small stinking spots on a Mississippi sidewalk. (18–19)

Horace's cumulative dismay at making the weekly trip to pick up fresh shrimp appears to have peaked, causing him to take what can be seen as constructive action. Belle Mitchell is never attractively characterized; on the other hand, Horace sounds unattractively like Emma Bovary in this passage.

Language also provides Horace with the means to deal with unromantic reality—he can divide himself in two. Self-division makes Horace his own commentator-observer, and this brief instance prepares for the more elaborate splits in Quentin, Darl and Gavin. Taking on the role of narrator puts a necessary distance between Horace and a painful situation; language makes emotion a part of objective reality. By describing the split, Horace makes his disillusionment more concrete. Much later in the novel, we learn that Horace will return to Belle, an act that epitomizes his acceptance of defeat. Horace's enactment of the stereotypic male crisis—entrapped by the female—identifies a cultural bias that will threaten Faulkner's capacity to reveal the other in language. Horace remains estranged from the female, his only authentic intimacy is in his own words. He finally writes to Belle, and the description of that writing emphasizes the connection between words and catharsis for Horace: "He sat at the table, looking down at the single page written neatly and illegibly over, feeling quiet and empty for the first time since he had found Popeye watching him across the spring four weeks ago" (*Sanctuary*, 274). He thinks, "I am sick to death for quiet," and again he comes closest to quiet through words. Horace's words are both neat and illegible, a paradox that underscores the one-sided nature of his letter writing. Just as he does with Narcissa, he writes ostensibly to communicate but finds in the act a more important means of self-communication and separation. We are never told what he writes, just what the writing does for him. Most important, the connections that Horace makes with other people mean the most to him when he writes or thinks about them.

Horace's love for language makes him suspect and certainly

futile in a world where concrete actions, however destructive, constitute reality. The narrators of both *Flags* and *Sanctuary* advance the perception of Horace as a bookish failure; both narrators also give bleak and violent accounts of this twentieth-century man's chances to take positive, redeeming action. Horace's ideals, nurtured by the books he loves and perpetuated by his own words, are responsible for his taking Lee Goodwin's case in *Sanctuary*. In the end, Horace's defeat in the courtroom comes when Narcissa proves the lie in Horace's characterization of her. The ancient codes of civilization mean nothing in a world with Popeye and lynch mobs and women who are not the sanctuaries of peace and perfection Horace wants them to be. Horace ultimately cannot make Narcissa the "bride of quietude" by saying that she is. His protest to Ruby Lamar, "Cant you see that perhaps a man might do something just because he knew it was right, necessary to the harmony of things that it can be done?" (290), is ineffective and empty in the face of events. Horace's defeat is in his refusal to accept other voices, his inability to relinquish language to the world that threatens to change it.

To a lesser degree, Faulkner also gets caught in the desire for an absolute language that he shares with Horace. Horace's defeat, however, serves as a warning voice. Particularly in *Flags*, we can see evidence that insofar as Horace's anxieties about the word are also a writer's anxieties, Faulkner begins to explore possible ways out of the problem of loss in language. The process is tentative, but to Horace's voice, Faulkner adds others, some of whom challenge the idea that words fix and preserve experience. In the writing of *Flags in the Dust*, in the creating of his own cosmos, Faulkner begins to mine the South and its history. This act reveals the connection he is beginning to make between language and its context. *Flags* marks Faulkner's first effort to unite his desire for authority as an author with his knowledge of the presence of the other in language. The effort is incomplete, in part because the two ideas may be irreconcilable and in part because so much of *Flags* is an elegy for the past.

The novel certainly mourns a past that memory and words can only represent; yet in the writing of that past, it very often becomes as real as the present. The entire Sartoris clan is raised on family legends and codes that nurture a way of life now disappearing but not gone. In the narrator's lush description of the Sartoris home, we can see how the language lingers over the past, both to mourn it and to preserve it:

> The stairway with its white spindles and red carpet mounted in a tall slender curve into upper gloom. From the center of the ceiling hung a chandelier of crystal prisms and shades, fitted originally for candles but since wired for electricity; to the right of the entrance, beside folding doors opened upon a room emanating an atmosphere of dim and seldom violated stateliness and known as the parlor, stood a tall mirror filled with grave obscurity like a still pool of evening water. At the end of the hallway checkered sunlight fell in a long slant across the door and the world was drowsily monotonous without, and from somewhere beyond the bar of sunlight a voice rose and fell in a rapid preoccupied minor, like a chant. The words were not always distinguishable, but Bayard Sartoris could not hear them at all. (*Flags*, 11–12)

The passage unfolds as a commemoration of the past that the house preserves. As the house materializes, details accumulate to encase us in the image of the grand old home—lived in yet filled with its grand past. That past and the telling of it is shaped by the values of the white Southern aristocracy.[34] The words work to preserve the house, wrapping it in drowsing sunlight and cherishing its "seldom violated stateliness." Then the present intrudes, in the form of a voice, as a deliberate revision of the nostalgic image before us. In his preoccupation, old Bayard is deliberately deaf to the voice; it violates the house's grandeur just as the present violates his idea of the world. The image of the past violated by a voice in the present is the model for the dialogue about language developing in the novel. The interrupting voice is Elnora's, the family's mulatto servant. The embodiment of the terrible lie in the grand and genteel Southern history, Elnora stands before Bayard Sartoris and us as evidence of Faulkner's recognition that other voices, here the black woman's, will always interrupt a given word. Bakhtin calls this phenomenon the internal dialogism of the spoken word: "Every word is directed toward an *answer* and cannot escape the profound influence of the answering word that it anticipates" ("Discourse in the Novel," 280). Unlike the poet who strips the word down to a single meaning and a narrow context, the novelist deals in discourse that is *of* the world, that exists in varied but concrete social and historical contexts. Faulkner begins to see the potential for power in novelistic language in *Flags*, but still he struggles with his yearning for a more absolute language.

The most explicit interruption of the past that everyone in the novel, including the narrator, elegizes is that of Caspey, Elnora's brother. Returned from the same war that leaves young Bayard and Horace bereft of peace and direction, Caspey is invigorated: " 'I dont take nothin' fum no white folks no mo. . . . War done changed all dat. If us colored folks is good enough to save France fum de Germans, den us is good enough to have de same rights de Germans has.' " (*Flags*, 63). But the weight of the past is heavy, nurtured even by his father Simon, the gentle Sartoris servant who knows his place and wants to stay there. When old Bayard demands that Caspey return to his, Caspey's rebellion soon dwindles to mutterings "just below Bayard's deafness" (86). The brief episode is capped with Simon's chiding words, " 'What us niggers want ter be free fer, anyhow? Aint we got ez many white folks now ez we kin suppo't?' " (87). Caspey remains silent for the rest of the book, replaced by the quiet, strangely romanticized voices of blacks whose dignity derives from the fact that they do not have power. Darwin Turner discusses Faulkner's attitude toward race in terms of the white schizophrenia that would allow him "to perceive the injustices of slavery but venerate the society which practiced it."[35] His point that Faulkner's black people reflect not only his sympathy and guilt but also his inability to understand the black perspective helps to explain the persistence of glorified endurance, writ large in Dilsey but present in most of Faulkner's blacks. It also reinforces my point that Faulkner's struggle with the other in language is most apparent in his depictions of blacks and women. But I do not suggest that Faulkner's despair over race was not genuine; in fact, his words tell us directly and obliquely that he was acutely aware of his own white voice.

When young Bayard is lost and taken in by the black family at Christmas, the narrator describes the group as "two opposed concepts antipathetic by race, blood, nature and environment, touching for a moment and fused within the illusion of a contradiction" (*Flags*, 393). The central anxiety of this novel is the problem of whether contradiction (the other) is an illusion or not. Caspey briefly contradicts the novel's dominant version of black people as ennobled by their inevitable station; his voice is evidence that Faulkner knew his own history also to be only a version of something gone and yet real. Recognizing the other is a kind of insurance against one's own deafness at the same time that it is a potential threat.

Bayard Sartoris' deafness and his refusal to accept the present are just as destructive as Horace's need to isolate experience in words. Yet Faulkner's reverence for the past and his belief in the power of language resonate through *Flags*. Like Horace Benbow and young Bayard Sartoris, Faulkner comes home in this novel and, like them, he must contend with its seductively romantic history. Sentence after sentence pushes back into time and uncovers ghosts it wants to revive. The brief description of the decrepit barn in which Suratt stashes his moonshine is typical of Faulkner's method: "The cavern of the hallway yawned in stale desolation—a travesty of earth's garnered fulness and its rich inferences" (144). The old barn is no longer used to store the fruits of harvest or to house animals but to hide liquor. It becomes in that sentence a symbol of the rich past that the entire novel mourns; yet in becoming that symbol, the barn also becomes one of life's "rich inferences." Language gives the old barn meaning, and the moonshine it houses loosens the tongue of Suratt, later to be renamed V. K. Ratliff, one of Faulkner's best raconteurs. Similarly, as often as Horace or Narcissa hides behind words, Will Falls or Aunt Jenny tells a story that brings "John [or Bayard] Sartoris into the room" (5). The evocative power of language can make the long-dead Sartoris, "freed as he was of time . . . a far more definite presence in the room than the two of them." Both the teller (Will Falls) and the listener (Bayard Sartoris) are for a time overshadowed by the past, by the man who is now literally of words. The freedom in conjuring John Sartoris is most surely felt by his author. In this novel, Faulkner writes about the past as something both dead and alive, glorious and dangerous. In doing so, he finds the way to explore his anxieties about the words that constitute it.

Horace Benbow is, of course, dogged by his fear that language is mutable and only representational throughout *Flags* especially, but the struggle between doubt and faith in the power of words invigorates Faulkner's writing. In *Flags*, Faulkner makes this struggle central to the resolution of his narrative. When Aunt Jenny learns that Narcissa has named her baby Benbow Sartoris instead of John, she snaps, "Do you think you can change one of 'em with a name?" (432), returning again to the novel's worry over the impotence of language. But then Aunt Jenny continues: "He [the Player, God?] must have a name for his pawns, though, but perhaps Sartoris is the name of the game itself—a game outmoded . . . for there is death in the sound of it" (433). Everything in the novel bears her out. She finishes by insisting on the power of the word, that the Sartoris name will doom the baby just as it did his father and all the other Sartoris men. Faulkner leaves Narcissa and Aunt Jenny then, enclosing them in a worded silence that echoes Horace's own desire: "Beyond the window evening was a windless lilac dream, foster-dam of quietude and peace" (433). Although Faulkner identifies the dangers of Horace's longing, he uses the same words to end the novel, making explicit his own desire to create "one almost perfect vase." In writing *Flags*, Faulkner both commemorates and condemns the South's history; it is the "almost" that invigorates an art that strives to be perfect or timeless.

Soon after the publication of *Sartoris*, Faulkner returned to Horace and his preoccupations in *Sanctuary*. Motivated perhaps by frustration at the nearly nonexistent readers, Faulkner professed to have churned out a story he hated because it pandered to popular appetites for sex and death.[36] But as many critics have argued, the book's obsession with sex and death connects it to *Flags*, *The Sound and the Fury*, and *As I Lay Dying*—all written and revised in the same four-year period. Whatever it shares with dimestore paperbacks, *Sanctuary* also gives Faulkner the opportunity to continue Horace's story, which is, in part, his own. Faulkner often called it a "potboiler," a story made up to make money, but his apparent distaste for the novel is also a significant revelation of his connection to Horace Benbow.

The world, and particularly the "reality" of the female, relentlessly threatens Horace Benbow's ideal of female innocence. That innocence is also threatened by his own sexuality, however repressed, but the primary threat is his own misguided worship of something that never existed in the first place. The corruption of female innocence is not just a problem for Horace. It is in the depiction of Temple Drake that we see most clearly how Faulkner closes off the text from the very voice it seeks to define, the female's. His text defines the female just as Horace does, even though Horace is written as a failure because of it. For whatever reasons, Faulkner does not open this novel to real dialogue; the shattering of Horace's ideal of the female is also the movement of the entire novel. The orientation upon which I base my reading of *Sanctuary* is Wayne Booth's discussion of what feminist criticism can tell us about Bakhtin's own failure to recognize the female voice in his criticism of Rabelais. Booth deals thoroughly and fairly with the troubling questions of intention and judgment which face both feminist and Bakhtinian critics alike. At the base of Booth's argument is the fact that Bakhtin's awareness of ideology in language makes the omission of a particular voice or ideology an issue whether the writer realizes it or not. Faulkner's fiction is fraught with his awareness of the female as other as much as it is preoccupied with female sexuality as a threatening presence in the lives of many of his male characters. In *Sanctuary*, images of sex and death merge in the figure of the female—particulary in Temple Drake.[37]

At the text's center is the rape of Temple Drake, but Horace's loss of innocence is the real focus of interest because Temple is never actually innocent in the first place. In *Sanctuary*, the idea of the female develops through Horace's honeysuckle-drenched thoughts of Little Belle; her flirtations with local boys pain him, as does her careless treatment of him, " 'It's just Horace' " (14). Even though Ruby listens to Horace's musings on the "conspiracy between female flesh and female season" which gives the illusion of innocence/spring/hope, and she passes what seems to be the correcting judgment, " 'He's crazy' " (15), nothing in the novel really argues with Horace's belief that the intellect—the male— creates the idea of innocence and then must protect itself from the natural but not innocent female force. Ruby herself, the good woman who only turns to "jazzing" to save her man, delivers the judgment of Temple that reinforces the novel's regret that women are not sanctuaries of innocence. Temple is a "doll-faced slut," a "hot little bitch" from the beginning (62, 64). That said, I do not agree with the many critics who argue simply that Temple wants to be raped, but I also think she is more than just a confused silly child. She is naive and vain, but the fact is that while her actions are unwitting, they are portrayed as *intrinsic to her gender*. And they, more than the man, are made responsible for the rape.

Faulkner's definition of female is inevitably the standard patriar-chal one, but his failure to imagine the female voice complicates his exploration of language as contextual and dependent upon the other.[38] Temple's coquetry, described as "taut, toothed" (51) incites Popeye's anger and the other male's lust as soon as she enters the scene. As frightened as she is by the rape, she has a confused but unmistakable knowledge that she has provoked the assault: " 'Something is happening to me! . . . I told you it was! . . . I told you all the time!' " (107). The strangeness of Temple's outcry veils the real horror—if she hasn't asked to be raped, she certainly knows it is inevitable. The experience is less a violation than an affirmation—Temple is Eve, the temptress disguised as the innocent.

After a quick recovery from the trauma, Temple becomes Po-peye's "girl" and resident of Miss Reba's Memphis brothel. When Horace finds her, he listens in horror to her account of the rape, told with "actual pride, a sort of naive and impersonal vanity" (226). We too listen in horror because in Temple Drake, Faulkner has written the dangerous Eve who taunts her would-be rapist with "Touch me! You're a coward if you dont" (229); innocence destroyed is not the real horror, the idea of woman presented here is. Her taunting presence reduces the ominous Popeye to sniveling and whimpering. One gets the uncomfortable feeling that if the corn cob had been a penis the horror would be mitigated. It seems that Ruby speaks the novel's truth when she accuses Temple of not knowing what it is to be wanted by a "real man" (the definitive "female" experience), that male impotence in the face of female sexuality (evil) is the real tragedy. Once female purity is unmasked for the sham that it is, the male is threatened. Horace identifies his own problem as a kind of impotence as well: " 'I lack courage: that was left out of me. The machinery is all here, but it wont run' " (18). Real men, like Lee Goodwin and Red have no illusions about women; they tame them with frequent and torrid sex, as in Temple's case, or with a baby and endless promises, as in Ruby's.

For all its sex and action, *Sanctuary* ultimately presents the world as Horace Benbow sees it: "a motionless ball in cooling space, across which a thick smell of honeysuckle writhed like cold smoke" (233–34). The scent of honeysuckle instantly triggers an association with female sexuality for Horace, as it does for Quentin Compson. The evil threat of female sexuality closes off this novel and makes it inferior to Faulkner's other work at this time. Contrary to Faulkner's apparent rationale, the novel's detective-story formula is not the real problem; withholding information to draw us into the story is one of Faulkner's favorite and most successful narrative strategies.[39] It even works here. The problem is that no authentic female voice is present and because the novel takes female sexuality as its central motif, the omission is a serious flaw.

Like the cold smoke in the image of female threat, Temple Drake "writhes," against men and walls alike, throughout the novel. The often-noted connection between Temple's name and her characterization reveals the lie of female purity that the novel seeks to expose. Temple is a word scrawled on bathroom walls, not whispered in reverence. The other women in *Sanctuary* are likewise defined in terms of their sexual threat. Little Belle is a budding coquette; Belle is an aging bit of used goods—" 'When you marry somebody else's wife, you start off ten years behind' " (17); Narcissa is the treacherous sister, the embodiment of repressed incestuous desire. The good or likeable women in the book are beyond sexuality either because of age (Aunt Jenny), obesity (Miss Reba), or motherhood (Ruby, Popeye's mother). But more damning than Faulkner's reliance on stereotypes is the novel's uninterrupted monologue on the connection between evil and death in the world and female sexuality. For all the critical attention given to archetypal evil in *Sanctuary*, very little has been paid to its female character. The end of the novel clarifies this connection. Horace Benbow has lost his case because of a woman's treachery. The lynch mob burns Lee Goodwin in terrible testament to the futility of Horace's words in this world. Now granted a horrible inversion of what he wants, Horace walks by the fire, unable to hear its "voice of fury like in a dream, roaring silently out of a peaceful void" (311). Defeated, he returns to Belle and, in the clear evidence of Little Belle's sexuality, is rendered inarticulate. Horace's silence is a kind of death, a more certain failure than even his worded illusions. Then we turn to Popeye who faces literal death, apparently without qualm. We are told of his end in the context of his pitiful childhood, wherein his pyromaniac grandmother and his strangely mechanical, sexually impotent adult self are vaguely connected. To give Popeye, the killer arrested on his yearly visit to mother, that particular childhood is to locate the reason for his behavior outside himself and in the female. Finally the novel closes on a sullen, unhappy Temple, taken away to Europe by her father the judge in a futile effort to protect or remove her from evil. The final image, seen through Temple's eyes, is of the sky "lying prone and vanquished in the embrace of the season of rain and death" just above where "dead tranquil queens in stained marble mused" (333). Much earlier in *Sanctuary*, before she is raped, Temple undresses and tries to sleep at the Old Frenchman place. She is described in language that prefigures the image of dead queens: "Temple lay, her hands crossed on her breast and her legs straight and close and decorous, like an effigy on an ancient tomb" (75). Silent and waiting, Temple lies in the dark while all about her men scramble to protect and to violate her. In the end, she looks, like the stained dead queens, upon the season of death that conquers the sky in a lover's embrace. The novel is no worded haven against the female threat, no sanctuary for innocence; instead, it closes itself inside its own fears that there is no safe place.

2

Quentin Compson: Isolation and the Power of Exchange

"I believe that every word a writing man writes is put down with the ultimate intention of impressing some woman that probably don't care anything at all for literature, as is the nature of women."—Dawson Fairchild in *Mosquitoes*

It did not matter to either of them which one did the talking, since it was not the talking alone which did it, performed and accomplished the overpassing, but some happy marriage of speaking and hearing wherein each before the demand, the requirement, forgave condoned and forgot the faulting of the other—faultings both in the creating of this shade whom they discussed (rather, existed in) and in the hearing and shifting and discarding the false and conserving what seemed true, or fit the preconceived— in order to overpass to love, where there might be paradox and inconsistency but nothing fault or false.—*Absalom, Absalom!*

Quentin Compson incorporates Horace Benbow's double-sided belief in the efficacy of language into a much larger, darker paradox. Quentin worries even more intensely and more obsessively over the communications he wants to make. Although he shares Horace's dreamy romanticism, Quentin is not as successfully socialized nor as experienced as he. Thus Quentin's communication concerns his emotional state much more exclusively. Quentin's emotional turmoil and his need to articulate it are inextricably and fatally linked. A firmly committed idealist, Quentin must wrestle with two absolute and opposite notions about language. He acknowledges and mourns what for him is the total disjunction between the word and its referent. He alternately denies any separation between word and referent at all. He is caught between his desire for language to create and to preserve experience and the implicit threat in his knowledge that if words empower him, they also empower others. The confusion that this paradox generates haunts Quentin until he dies.

The often-noted connection between Quentin's tortured consciousness and his convoluted language is vital to an understanding of his section in *The Sound and the Fury*. Near the end of his final day, Quentin plays out the last in a series of imaginary conversations with his father. All day he has walked and listened to the voices in his head; the following passage encompasses all the major aspects of his relationship to language. He begins by insisting on the truth of his story of incest with Caddy:

> i wasnt lying i wasnt lying and he you wanted to sublimate a piece of natural folly into a horror and then exorcise it with truth and i it was to isolate her out of the loud world so that it would have to flee us of necessity and then the sound of it would be as though it had never been and he did you try to make her do it and i i was afraid she might and then it wouldnt have done any good but if I could tell you we did it would have been so and the others wouldnt be so and then the world would roar away and he now this other you are not lying now either but you are still blind to what is in yourself to that part of general truth the sequence of natural events and their causes which shadows every mans brow even benjys you are not thinking of finitude you are contemplating an apotheosis . . . you cannot bear to think that someday it will no longer hurt you like this.[1]

Here Quentin fully articulates the desire to enshrine a sister's purity that we first see in Horace. Both men believe their words can create and preserve a permanent innocence in which their sisters can dwell. Both men also find comfort and greater expression in their internal monologues; spoken language is far more threatening. Of more central importance than the impulse toward purity is the fact that Quentin is responsible for all of this conversation.

Quentin arrives at the hypothetical dialogue with his father by first associating Harvard's chimes with the deliberate and irrevocable effect he wishes he could have on other people. The clear, "serenely peremptory" chimes possess the authority he wants. He then associates this longing with his discovery of Caddy's loss of innocence because that is his primary obsession. He experiences Caddy's sexual encounter "just by imagining," and straightaway he moves from the highly charged spectre of "swine untethered in pairs rushing coupled" to an analysis of his reaction to it. The voice Quentin calls "he" carries Mr. Compson's unmistakable ring of jaded authority, but we have no reason to believe Quentin is not imagining this dialogue as well. In fact, we have clear evidence that he is. Throughout, when recalling his father's actual words, Quentin prefaces them with "Father said." He does not do so here. Because Quentin invests all sexuality, and certainly incest, with such horror, and because all of his previous mentions of incest have been fragmented interruptions of other thoughts, it is unlikely that he ever risked giving the word utterance.

Also, Faulkner has confirmed that Quentin never actually told the incest story to his father. In explaining Quentin's motives, Faulkner illuminates a part of Quentin's belief in language: "He said . . . if I would say this to my father, whether it was a lie or not . . . maybe he would answer back the magic word which would relieve me of this anguish . . . would it help me, would it clarify, would I see clearer what it is that I anguish over?"[2] To a great extent, then, Quentin's imaginary dialogues are his attempts to articulate and thus to understand his emotional pain. But because the dialogues are actually doublings of interior, solipsistic imaginings, they trap Quentin more securely in internal cogitating and increase his pain by refusing him any external help. Quentin's attempt to preempt the presence of another voice by creating his father's words himself fails not because he cannot reproduce Mr. Compson's voice (he has listened well all of his life) but because the very presence of another's words threatens his own. In Bakhtin's terms, Quentin cannot reconcile his desire for the power and safety of monologic language with his knowledge that all language exists in the world and the world exists in language. Implicit in Quentin's attempt is his desire to believe that the articulation is the reality. The incest story itself and his need for the "magic word" from his father exemplifies that faith.

But Quentin also tests his belief, through the guise of his father's voice, by exposing the lie and even assigning motives for it. The value for him lies in the exchange itself. Quentin generates both sides of the conversation to clarify the paradox with which he is wrestling. The issue centers not on Caddy but on Quentin's struggle with words and the absolute truth he wants them to hold. The dialectic reveals that Quentin's growing isolation is teeming with thought and concerns relational possibilities; it also reinforces the fact that Quentin's real life is in his mind. He can keep the world at bay and yet populate his internal world as he wishes. The link between Quentin's problems and the medium through which he can articulate them is strong. The previous passage touches on Faulkner's notions about language that inform Quentin's narratives in both *The Sound and the Fury* and *Absalom, Absalom!*: Quentin believes that words give control and create truth or reality; at the same time, he knows that words are not the same as their referents.

Quentin again defends his incest story, this time revealing his reason for wanting to tell it, when he says: "if i could tell you we did it would have been so." In Quentin's words, we can hear the unmistakable echo of Horace's desire to control circumstances through language, and they corroborate Horace's claim that lying is an effort to survive. The incest lie is the most notable example of Quentin's belief that saying something makes it so. That he creates the story in an attempt to isolate Caddy and to recover lost time is an important, much-explored critical issue. But Quentin can only do this through language, and that fact puts words to the complicated test of Faulkner's "educated half-madman."[3] Quentin's lie effects the same results as the noisy plans of the boys he observes "making of unreality a possibility, then a probability, then an incontrovertible fact, as people will when their desires become words" (*Sound and Fury*, 145).[4] Faulkner tells us directly

⁀in the appendix what is implied in the text itself, that Quentin does not desire Caddy sexually, nor does he love the *idea* of incest, but that he wants the word to work its effect on his father. Then, "he, not God, could by that means cast himself and his sister both into hell" (411). With the word he would wield a power as great as God's; nothing else he has in his grasp can equal that.

In both *The Sound and the Fury* and *Absalom, Absalom!*, Faulkner connects Quentin's troubled desire for the power of the word to his troubled relation with his father. And in *Absalom*, we learn that his grandfather as well fostered his doubts and his faith in words. As he recounts Thomas Sutpen's efforts to learn Haitian, Quentin remembers his grandfather's definition of language as

> that meager and fragile thread . . . by which the little surface corners and edges of men's secret and solitary lives may be joined for an instant now and then before sinking back into the darkness where the spirit cried for the first time and was not heard and will cry for the last time and will not be heard then either.[5]

The definition is strikingly bleak because it establishes an immediate and primal relationship between language and the human condition and then declares that relationship tenuous at best. At the same time that language is deemed essential, it is defined as poor help indeed. In *The Sound and the Fury*, Quentin remembers hearing his grandfather and Colonel Sartoris: "They were always talking and Grandfather was always right" (219). In light of Grandfather's view of language, this report of his verbal authority appears contradictory, but the incongruity here establishes a precedent for the complications in Quentin's relationship with language.

That precedent is established more firmly in Quentin's relationship with his father. In *The Sound and the Fury*, Mr. Compson does a great deal of explaining and defining for his son. Much of his speech is aphoristic, as if he intends to condense life to a series of maxims: "Victory is an illusion of philosophers and fools" (93); "time is a symptom of mind-function" (94), "Purity is a negative state . . . tragedy is second-hand" (143), and the famous comment on time as the "reducto absurdum of human experience" (105). The phrases punctuate Quentin's monologue with snippets of "truth" that continually say no. And therein lies the paradox with which Quentin has had to deal all of his life. Mr. Compson's words, which convey a relentless nihilism, are spoken in a way that shows his belief in the power of words. Thus it makes perfect sense that Quentin should want to tell his father the incest story and then imagine his exposing it as a lie. It is through his father's rejection of the story that Quentin must confront the discrepancy between word and referent. Quentin realizes that saying he committed incest is a lie and therefore is ineffective. Although the lie is as close as Quentin wants to come to the reality of the experience, he never actually tells it. He doesn't because then he would have to deal directly with the gap between the word and the reality of the experience it names. Instead, he tortures himself with the knowledge that there is a gap. Twice in the novel he remembers the void left by his mother's self-absorption in terms of his need to say her name. As he cleans his bloodstained tie in preparation to drown himself, he thinks, *"if I'd just had a mother so I could say Mother Mother"* (213) and makes her name an aborted cry for help. The fact that he cannot say the word indicates that he knows he cannot create reality—the word is too frail to conjure the maternal comfort he needs. Again Quentin approaches experience as something he either can or cannot put into words.

The frailty of language stands before Quentin, a dangerous obstacle that makes his presence at Harvard an ontological problem. Near the end of his day, he contemplates dying in terms of elementary grammar: "I am. Drink. I was not" (*Sound and Fury*, 216). He makes the idea real to himself by saying it, but that leads him to the reason he is in Cambridge: "Harvard is such a fine sound forty acres is no high price for a fine dead sound" (217). Aside from the pain he feels for his brother's loss, Quentin plays with the idea that he will be dead at Harvard by pointing up the emptiness of the word itself. Selling the pasture was a wasted effort because Quentin will be dead and Harvard is a dead word. Harvard no longer means anything; as a word it is without function. Quentin's suspicion of the abstract word aligns Faulkner with the widespread distrust of abstraction found in much of the literature of the 1920s.[6] By relegating Harvard itself to the emptiness of abstraction, Quentin condemns all intellectual pursuits. He of course learns about the lack of meaning in scholastic endeavor from his father. Quentin tells us that Mr. Compson describes Harvard as the place "where the best of thought . . . clings like dead ivy vines upon old dead brick" (*Sound and Fury*, 117–18). The allusion to Matthew Arnold's declaration that literary criticism must function "to propagate the best that is known and thought in the world" underscores the bitter end to which Mr. Compson believes faith in words has brought us.[7] In Compson's sardonic assessment, Faulkner also challenges Arnold's elitism as creating a deadening intellectual monologue. But Mr. Compson also makes his point very effectively by depending upon his audience's knowledge of the very idea he disparages. Here the allusion to literature has the same double-sided effect of the literary allusions in *Flags in the Dust*.

While Mr. Compson's penchant for cleverly phrased bits of defeatism may weaken his credibility with us, Quentin takes his father seriously. Both father and son see Mr. Compson as the authority. In one re-created conversation with his father about virginity, Quentin thinks of sex as a foreign language: "O That That's Chinese I dont know Chinese" (*Sound and Fury*, 143). As he moves from his own virginity to Caddy's sexual experience, his father tells him:

> Purity is a negative state and therefore contrary to nature. It's nature is hurting you not Caddy and I said That's just words and he said So is virginity and I said you dont know. You cant know and he said Yes. On the instant when we come to realize that tragedy is second-hand. (143)

This dialogue allows Quentin to analyze his anguish in the terms most fundamental to the problem itself.[8] By equating sexuality with Chinese, Quentin establishes his frame of reference as unequivocally linguistic. He then pulls the frame apart by declaring his father's arguments "just words." This maneuver allows Mr. Compson to challenge his son's reverence for virginity, and Quen-

tin's strategy dissolves into ineffective denial. Quentin is an abso-
lutist; words are empty yet meaningful. Meanwhile his father has
the last word. Mr. Compson illustrates the paradox as well. If
nothing means anything, as he says, then words have a privileged
position because they can describe nothing. Quentin sees his own
belief in the power and the substance of words as erroneous, but
he cannot accept this conclusion. If he could, he would then nullify
his life's efforts—to articulate experience. He continually plays
out variations of this debate as he moves through his day.

When Mr. Compson recognizes his son's idealized concept of
virginity, he locates the primary symptom of Quentin's problem
as a belief in an empty term. Exposure of the incest story repeats
Mr. Compson's stripping away of Quentin's futile belief in the
truth of words, but this time Quentin is not repeating an actual
conversation. In imagined conversation, he assigns to his father
the phrase: "You are not thinking of finitude you are contemplating
an apotheosis" (*Sound and Fury*, 220). Language not only can
create an ideal, it can preserve it. Or that is what part of Quentin
Compson wants to believe. He wants to yank Caddy out of the
"loud world" with the words he can never utter, for if he did, they
would make his desire impossible. A disoriented idealist, he moves
between wanting words to create and preserve forever and fearing
they can do nothing. John Irwin interprets Quentin's act of narration as a means of achieving authorial control over time as well as
his father. In doing so, the critic rightly identifies Quentin's reliance on language as a need to create, to be original.[9] Irwin's
treatment of *Absalom, Absalom!* offers provocative discussion of
Quentin's desire to achieve priority over his father, or "authority
through originality" (113). I want to underscore Quentin's strong
connection to the act of authoring and to redirect Irwin's emphasis
on Quentin's psychology to this character's relationship with language. Quentin knows that language affords a certain control and
that his father is a man of words.

Issues of Quentin and authorship in *Absalom* apply as well to
The Sound and the Fury, where, in one of his more cryptic flashes
of thought, Quentin also identifies the control that language brings
him: "*Say it to Father will I will am my father. Progenitive I*

invested him created I him Say it to him it will not be for he will
say I was not and then you and I since philoprogenitive" (152).
Here his plea to Caddy to tell their father that she is pregnant
widens to include the power struggle Quentin conducts with his
father. Unpunctuated fragments underscore the passage's ambiguity as his talk about Caddy's pregnancy merges into the idea of
creating his father. The word *progenitive* is a form of *progenitor*,
or the originator of a line of descent. The idea that Quentin is, in
his thoughts, creating his father interrupts his directive to Caddy.
The phrase "created I him" is either elliptic, in which case Quentin
means he created himself as well, or syntactically convoluted, in
which case he means simply that he created his father. The ambiguity keeps possibility alive. The fact that he moves from one kind
of creation to another demonstrates the power Quentin invests in
language, for he can create his father only figuratively in words.

The sentence, "Say it to him it will not be for he will say I was
not," suggests several interpretations. Quentin could mean that if
Caddy tells their father she is pregnant—now with Quentin's
child—he will make her *not* pregnant by saying that Quentin did
not commit incest. Or perhaps he means that Mr. Compson would
say Quentin is not his son, and the disinheritance would allow him
to take Caddy away. The phrase "since philoprogenitive" then
refers to Mr. Compson, for Quentin and Caddy could leave because
their father would still have Jason and Benjy. Or more radically,
Quentin could mean that his father would say literally that he does
not exist. In all three readings, Quentin gives a greater power to
his father, but with the third, he gives him the ultimate, killing
power. Mr. Compson can declare Caddy no longer pregnant, Quentin no longer his son, or Quentin no longer alive. In Quentin's
apparent wish to be disowned and to run away is the fear that to
be disowned is to be dissolved. Language is indeed potent.

But in *The Sound and Fury*, Quentin's assertions of creativity,
and for the power of language, once again meet with opposition in
the form of his father's greater control. And Quentin himself creates the scenario, albeit fragmentary. The incest story and Mr.
Compson's words both come from Quentin, whose involvement
with language is as basic as his need to create. What Quentin

actually creates here is one variation of the theoretical debate that he continually pursues. Mr. Compson embodies the negative side of the argument that speaks for the frailty of language, which threatens always to topple Quentin's belief in the ideal, absolute world language can create. Quentin's continual return to the same argument speaks both to its importance and to his inability to accept the verdict he assigns to his father. From the first time Quentin articulates the incest lie in his mind, we can see that this is a power struggle for him: "*I have committed incest I said Father it was I it was not Dalton Ames* And when he put Dalton Ames. Dalton Ames. When he put the pistol in my hand I didn't" (97–98). Dalton Ames' name repeatedly interferes with the completion of a sentence that mirrors Quentin's inability to act on his desire. The name, even as a word, competes with Quentin's attempt to make language equivalent to action. Dalton Ames, then, is both a disruptive stutter and a litany Quentin repeats often, thus keeping his fear and pain active. At one point Quentin reflects on the symbol he has made: "Dalton Ames. It just missed gentility. Theatrical fixture. Just papier-mache, then touch. Oh. Asbestos. Not quite bronze" (113). The name affords Quentin a brief opportunity to exercise some control over the man. His condescension about Ames' name illustrates exactly Quentin's method. He feels much more comfortable with the name of his rival than with the man himself. In fact, he correlates the name directly with the actual man.

The correlation allows Quentin to articulate his hostility through a linguistic maneuver, and Dalton Ames' name reveals him to be relatively unsubstantial. Quentin's hostility gives him the only form of power he has against Ames: "What a picture of Gerald I to be one of the *Dalton Ames oh asbestos Quentin has shot* background. . . . Telling us about Gerald's women in a *Quentin has shot Herbert he shot his voice through the floor of Caddy's room* tone of smug approbation" (*Sound and Fury*, 130). Twice Quentin's thoughts of his sister's suitors interrupt his narrative about the womanizing Gerald Bland. The passage emphasizes the tangled but strong contradictions between his sexual fears and his anger. Quentin thinks of people as voices—they and their words are one for him.[10] Thus Quentin imagines shooting Herbert's *voice*. If he can stop Herbert from talking about wedding plans, then perhaps the fact of his marriage to Caddy will go away. Faulkner then complicates matters by introducing a deliberate ambiguity. The phrase "he shot his voice" could also mean that Quentin conceives of his own voice as a weapon with which he can destroy Herbert, thus assigning the voice a killing power. Eight pages later Faulkner clears away the ambiguity with the sentence "Quentin has shot all of their voices through the floor of Caddy's room." But by allowing the alternative reading to exist at all, Faulkner keeps alive Quentin's beliefs that language gives control and gives nothing.

Although Quentin's control over the world of words grows increasingly fragile, it never fails him as profoundly as when he recreates his encounter with Ames: "Then I heard myself saying Ill give you until sundown to leave town" (*Sound and Fury*, 198). He can do no more than parrot this trite and inane challenge to battle. Quentin further detaches himself from his words when he tells Dalton his name: "My mouth said it I didnt say it at all" (198). At this point, Dalton has taken control of the conversation by asking questions. Quentin's fear at losing control causes him to dissociate himself from his own body. When faced with the undeniable reality of Dalton Ames, he cannot put words together effectively. His emotional pain pushes him from the safety of the world of the mind into the terrifying world of actual confrontation. His words turn into parody and expose the flaw in his belief in the efficacy of words. They do not help him against Dalton Ames, but nothing does.

The name still does have power, as Caddy shows him when she makes him put his hand against her throat and say Dalton's name: "I felt the first surge of blood there it surged in strong accelerating beats" (*Sound and Fury*, 203). When Caddy makes Quentin feel the power that the name possesses, she demonstrates a keen understanding of her brother. The gesture forces Quentin to confront the reality of his sister's sexual awakening and underscores the fact that words are most literally the link between Quentin's interior world and objective reality. Caddy also challenges Quentin's faith in words, asking *"do you want me to say it do you think that if I say it it wont be"* (151), but Quentin will not stop fighting for the power of the word. He recalls the desperate attempt of his wish to make Caddy his partner in the incest lie: *"I'll tell you how it was I'll tell Father then itll have to because you love Father then we'll have to go away amid the pointing and the horror the clean flame I'll make you say we did"* (185). All that matters is that they *say* it happened; the words will be the reality.

Quentin knows very well the power that telling holds. He observes that the Deacon, Harvard's old black eccentric, has told of graduating from divinity school so often that he believes he did. Quentin pays tribute to the power of the word, but he does so with the implicit, sardonic recognition that he is as guilty as the Deacon of turning a lie into the truth simply by telling it. He understands, as does Horace, that words allow people to alter circumstance. Again Quentin pushes at the line between lie and truth, testing the potency of language. Similarly *Absalom, Absalom!* is full of references to the power of telling. The first time Miss Rosa tells Quentin of Thomas Sutpen, her words act on him: "Her voice would not cease, it would just vanish. . . . the voice not ceasing but vanishing into and then out of the long intervals. . . . Out of the quiet thunderclap he [Sutpen] would abrupt" (4). Synesthesia, oxymoron, and an invented verb show language to be both beautiful and accurate in creating the dreamlike verisimilitude that Quentin experiences. As he becomes immersed in Miss Rosa's story, the conditional past tense (*would cease*) is replaced with the present participle (*ceasing*)—the experience, which is out of the past and hypothetical, grows more immediate and more real until, like John Sartoris in *Flags*, Thomas Sutpen takes form.

The Power of Narration

Invention through narration, a central motif in *Absalom*, is an act of power, and it is one that Quentin most fears and is most attracted to. His fears about narration come out of his belief in the power of language. More specifically, Quentin is a reluctant listener to other's narratives because he knows their power to ensnare, even to engulf him. Probably because of this, his own narration is charged with partially repressed emotion. And his collaboration with Shreve is not an easy achievement; he protests Shreve's interruptions with " 'Wait, I tell you . . . I am telling' " (345). For Quentin, narrating is the act of asserting a self that is filled with unarticulated, warring fears and desires. By this time— Quentin is telling of Sutpen's meeting with Henry to discuss Bon and Judith—Quentin's stake in the narrative has increased to the point that the telling has become as vital as the story itself.

Faulkner prepares us for this from the novel's beginning. Soon after he first listens to Miss Rosa, Quentin's imagination interacts with her words and transports him into the past. Early on, we learn how the narrative works on him:

> It (the talking, the telling) seemed (to him, to Quentin) to partake of that logic- and reason-flouting quality of a dream which the sleeper knows must have occurred, stillborn and complete, in a second, yet the very quality upon which it must depend to move the dreamer (verisimilitude) to credulity—horror or pleasure or amazement—depends as completely upon a formal recognition of and acceptance of elapsed and yet-elapsing time as music or a printed tale. (*Absalom*, 22–23)

The sentence crystallizes the tension between Quentin's ideas of language as both in and out of a larger, potentially altering context. Words work an inexplicable, dreamlike effect that depend upon an awareness of time's passage to make them acceptable, or real. They are "stillborn and complete," a phrase which evokes creation, unity, and death all at once, and ultimately the words move him to live another life in his imagination. That life is so powerful that Quentin describes it as blurring the line between dream and reality: "It was all the same, there was no difference: waking or sleeping" (464). When Quentin thinks of how his grandfather told him that Judith Sutpen brought Charles Bon's letter to his grandmother, he can see it happen. He thinks, "*I have heard too much, I have been told too much; I have had to listen to too much, too long* thinking *Yes, Shreve sounds almost exactly like father: that letter*" (259–60). The story threatens to engulf him;

just the memory of his father's words can pull him into the imagined life. He says—in three ways—that he has listened too long. The repetition underscores both his meaning and the pattern of building a narrative that the novel establishes.

In addition to the power that the narrative itself has, the voice of Quentin's roommate begins to sound like his father's. Later Quentin thinks, *"Maybe nothing ever happens once and is finished. . . . maybe Father and I are both Shreve, maybe it took father and me both to make Shreve or Shreve and me both to make Father or maybe Thomas Sutpen to make all of us"* (*Absalom,* 326–27). Quentin is talking about narration and about connections among people, even across generations. He theorizes that it is not events that connect people, but what people make of events that connects them. In the process, they also make each other, and they accomplish all of this through language. Articulation allows humans a tremendous power, but it involves certain, equally great risks. Faulkner shows us how the collaborative effort of telling the life of Thomas Sutpen, for example, has worked to shape and to distinguish the people who tell it as well. The human will to gain authority always poses a threat to the idea of collaboration; Faulkner structures both the novels around a series of retellings that vie for authority. Just as Quentin must contend with the word of his father, each retelling must contend with the one previous to it. In doing so, they become, in Bakhtin's words, "internally persuasive discourse" ("Discourse in the Novel," 342). Bakhtin frames his definition of this discourse in terms of the struggle of individual discourse, inseparable as it is from individual ideology, with the word of an authority. The same kind of struggle occurs in the novel as author and characters alike compete with authoritative discourse to make a text their own. For Faulkner, the authoritative discourse is that of his literary predecessors, particularly the legacy of Southern rhetoric, and his own acknowledged impulse to write authoritative discourse. He fights that impulse through characters who must contend with different versions of Sutpen's story, and most significantly, through Quentin, who allows Faulkner to confront directly the dangers of closed, monologic narrative.

Collaboration also involves the dissolving of separate identity, and Quentin's speculations include the darker notion that too much telling threatens to erase the self.

At the beginning of *Absalom, Absalom!*, Quentin seemingly divides himself in two, for much the same reason that Horace Benbow does in *Sanctuary*—when his emotional investment is very high, the intellect splits off and observes the pain. Part of Quentin is a member of the ghost-filled South, and another part is the young man preparing to go to Harvard University. Both selves are compelled to listen to Miss Rosa; for a moment they talk to one another "in the long silence of notpeople, in notlanguage" (*Absalom*, 5). We then see Quentin's thoughts. One self paraphrases Miss Rosa's words, while the other self embellishes with parenthetical comments. Although it is labeled "notlanguage," the exchange is far clearer than most of Quentin's musings in *The Sound and the Fury*. The principle difference in the Quentin of *Absalom* is that he is less trapped inside his own monologic nightmare. Other people, living and dead, participate more fully in his narratives in *Absalom*. He is of course still tortured by that, but his life is not threatened. However, Quentin's method, internal debate, is characteristic. The act of recasting helps him to clarify his connection to Miss Rosa's story. An important element in the opening pages of *Absalom* is the effect of her words on Quentin. We know that his childhood memories reverberate with the names out of the past that Miss Rosa is recalling: "His very body was an empty hall echoing with sonorous defeated names; he was not a being, an entity, he was a commonwealth" (9). The image of Quentin as a place waiting to be filled explains why the story can affect him so powerfully.

As the novel continues, nothing more is said directly of Quentin's divided self. Reconstructing the past takes precedence over all else, but throughout the telling we see Quentin struggle with what the legacy means for him. We are told that Quentin's voice has a "tense suffused restrained quality" (345), that it is "flat, curiously dead" (322). These descriptions in *Absalom* are scant, but they go far in suggesting Quentin's tremendous inner struggle. His voice is even described once as "repressed" (273), and certainly when he speaks the novel's final words, we know the story has been about much more than Thomas Sutpen: *"I dont hate it* (the South) he thought, panting in the cold air, the iron New England dark; *I dont. I dont! I dont hate it! I dont hate it!"* (471). The vehemence of his denial indicates how deeply he has been affected; the South is obviously a key part of who Quentin is. Quentin's denial is part of his attempt to deny that language exists in social and historical contexts. He tries to detach himself from the story by telling Shreve to "wait." His dread at hearing it all again and again lies just below his quiet exterior, until finally he can only refuse, mechanically, the horror. The issue is not whether all the words that make up the story are factually verifiable, but whether existence is what we say it is. Believing that it is, Quentin can divide himself, he and Shreve can become interchangeable, and as they talk and listen, they can even become Henry and Bon. The division in Quentin measures the intensity of his conflict, the enormous struggle he undergoes as words blur the line between illusion and reality. But Quentin makes a commitment to the narrative act. The hypothesizing, explaining, and simple articulation are for Quentin both essential and difficult.

He finds the experience difficult because it also confronts him again with his own anguish. It is clearly significant that the incestuous overtone of the Henry-Judith-Bon story is the subject of Quentin's narrative. And the terror of miscegenation, embodied in Henry Sutpen, is equally a part of the ugly "something" through which Quentin cannot pass.[11] But Quentin also narrates the story of Thomas Sutpen's youth—in which, armed with a message from his father, the boy Sutpen is denied entrance to the plantation owner's home, takes the rebuff as a denial of his very existence, and executes the first step of his grand design to establish himself as a presence. The letter Quentin receives from his father, apparently announcing Miss Rosa's death, is the catalyst. His re-creation comes out of what Sutpen told his grandfather, but Quentin says several times that Sutpen was neither a talker nor a listener. Thus Quentin tells of a man who seems different from him in the most important way.

Quentin's Sutpen does not listen to the "vague and cloudy tales of Tidewater splendor" (277) that he could have made a part of his childhood. The words were unconnected to what he saw around him, so he dismissed him. Existence as a poor tenant farmer's son fell far short of "splendor." Nothing could be more foreign to Quentin Compson, who takes the myth of his Southern heritage for his own reality. The undelivered message triggers Sutpen's realization that neither he nor his words mean anything: "*I not only wasn't doing any good to him by telling it or any harm to him by not telling it, there ain't any good or harm either in the living world that I can do to him*" (296–97). In Sutpen, Faulkner brings Quentin face to face with the embodiment of his desire to acknowledge no dialogue in language. Quentin makes it clear that what is, in essence, Sutpen's freedom from the word sets him in motion to create his own present and future. Quentin makes a connection between Sutpen's terseness and his ability to act decisively. Sutpen is a man of action, but Quentin turns the action back into words; he tells of what Sutpen *does*, but he always centers his narrative on what he *says*, how he says it, and what he does not say.

Sutpen's revelations to Quentin's grandfather clearly establish that he favored bare facts over narrative complexity. So Quentin creates it for him:

> He went to the West Indies. That's how Sutpen said it: not how he managed to find where the West Indies were, not where ships departed from to go there, nor how he got to where the ships were and got in one, nor how he liked the sea, nor about the hardships of a sailor's life and it must have been hardship indeed for him, a boy of fourteen or fifteen who had never seen the ocean before, going to sea in 1823. He just said, "So I went to the West Indies." (*Absalom*, 299)

By reminding us of all that Sutpen's one sentence omits, Quentin makes him alive, even sympathetic. We listen to Quentin's words and learn who Sutpen was. He also supplies Sutpen's motivation for telling his grandfather of his "design": "trying hard to explain now because now he was old and knew it, knew it was being old that he had to talk against" (325). The need to order experience and fight time through words touches even Sutpen. Indeed Quentin describes Sutpen's own speech as full of "bombastic phrases" (299); he wore a Confederate uniform that "fitted itself to the swaggering of all his gestures and to the forensic verbiage in which he stated calmly . . . the most simple and the most outrageous things" (307). Quentin establishes Sutpen, through his habit of speech, as active, manipulative, concerned with appearances or his design, rather than with complex motives or understanding. Quentin's Sutpen is almost childlike in his single-minded devotion to his plan.

Quentin devotes considerable time establishing Sutpen's rationality in negative terms. He notes several times that Sutpen had little regard for establishing continuity or even explanations for what he tells the elder Compson:

> He was telling it all over and still it was not absolutely clear—the how and why he was here and what he was—since he was not talking about himself. He was telling a story. He was not bragging about something he had done; he was just telling a story about something a man named Thomas Sutpen had experienced, which would still have been the same story if the man had no name at all; if it had been told about any man at all over whiskey at night. (*Absalom*, 308-9)

Quentin offers this explanation calmly and with apparent understanding. Quentin says that Sutpen is telling a story, and yet he has no regard for sequence or any of the transitions that a narrator usually employs *because* he or she is telling a story. Sutpen understands nothing about narrative; thus Quentin must give the skeleton substance. Quentin's words order and connect the pieces of Sutpen's life. He does see Sutpen's relationship with language as essentially negative and foreign to his own, but he also notes Sutpen's untroubled acceptance of something with which he must struggle. In the preceding passage, Quentin is describing the detachment of a narrator who is turning experience into words. Sutpen can mythologize himself with ease, largely because he relies on words only to recall action. Language is simply utile for him, whereas words compose the very fabric of Quentin's life. Because words give form to the thoughts and monologues from

Quentin's murky psyche, he views Sutpen's simple detachment from the words that form his experiences as a mysterious achievement.

The connections that Quentin makes in his narrative of Sutpen and those he makes about his own obsessions do not help him communicate with other people. That brief time when he and Shreve narrate together in a "happy marriage of speaking and hearing" (*Absalom*, 395) is the closest that Quentin comes to letting go of his desire for the absolute word.[12] Even more acutely than Horace Benbow, Quentin believes that words preserve as long as they aren't spoken. Utterance turns them loose in the public realm where other voices can defile them. As he tells the incest story, he knows his father will tear it away from him. As he tells the Sutpen story, he knows that Shreve will interrupt and alter and push him to confront his own troubled connections to it. Both the telling of his meeting with Henry Sutpen and Shreve's surprise question, "Why do you hate the South?" (471), bring Quentin across the final threshold. The trap appears complete. Language creates experience, but language is also communal and thus mutable. But Quentin retains one method of escape before he silences himself forever.

Silence, as an image and an idea, runs through all narrative connected with Quentin. In *Absalom*, he yearns for the power that telling gives but still sees other's telling as a threat to him. Just after he has told of meeting Henry Sutpen and acknowledging that for him it means "nevermore of peace" (465), Quentin temporarily reaches the isolation and silence that he believes language can achieve. He and Shreve have come to the end of their story; Quentin imagines Miss Rosa watching the Sutpen house burn, "struggling and fighting like a doll in a nightmare, making no sound" (468). Shreve makes a comment about "Aunt Rosa" returning to town, and we learn that "Quentin did not answer; he did not even say *Miss Rosa*. He just lay there staring at the window without even blinking, breathing the chill heady pure snow-gleamed darkness" (468–69). Quentin has no words; he does not need them. The story has brought him to its full, soundless horror. The "snow-gleamed darkness" mirrors the state of his mind. But only briefly does the horror hang there silently, for Shreve's voice intrudes, and finally Quentin's own frantic denial of it ends the novel.

The Power of Silence

To a greater extent, Quentin continues to see the human voice as threatened or threatening in *The Sound and the Fury*. Its absence, silence, is both a haven and a reminder of Quentin's own failure to speak.[13] On his last trip to his dormitory, Quentin takes a drink of water that leaves *"the taste of dampened sleep in the long silence of the throat"* (216), thus connecting water to his eternal silence through death. Here Quentin sees himself alive as a disturber of silence; he continues "up the corridor, waking the lost feet in whispering battalions in the silence . . . And then I'll not be. The peacefullest words. Peacefullest words. *Non fui. Sum. Fui. Non sum"* (216). Quentin's death wish and his struggle against the passage of time merge, and he anticipates the moment when he will have eternal peace and silence. He contemplates this through the repetition of the Latin words for "I am" and "I was"— language makes his decision real. Quentin displays a less elaborate version of what will be Darl Bundren's and Gavin Stevens' fascination with translating the idea of time into verb tenses. But in this instance, Quentin seems to find the words soothing rather than a mark of his failure, or perhaps he is just tired of listening to the voices in his head.

Quentin actually speaks very little. In *Absalom, Absalom!* he listens through at least three-quarters of the novel, although he is the only character present throughout. In *The Sound and the Fury*, he avoids talking to Shreve as often as he can, and when he goes before the justice, he lets Shreve and Spoade explain that he did not harm the little girl he calls sister. He attempts simple conversation with the young boy he meets in the country and of course with "sister," who is "serene and secret" (160). Neither child ever speaks to him. Quentin also notices silence; his descriptions of it are among the most lucid and lyrical passages in his section. He finds silence in nature and in it comes as close to peace as he ever does: "The sound of the bees diminished, sustained yet, as though instead of sinking into silence, silence merely increased between us, as water rises" (153). Silence, then, is an entity by which Quentin measures his separateness from the rest of the world. He thinks of himself as surrounded by it when he runs away from Benjy's inarticulate but loud pain at Caddy's loss of virginity: "crickets sawing away in the grass pacing me with a small travelling island of silence" (186). His own memories of Caddy hinge on associations with nature (honeysuckle, water, twilight), and he taunts himself with "the voice that breathed o'er eden" (130).

In the present, however, nature seems less threatening and reflects Quentin's own state of mind: "Even sound seemed to fail in this air, like the air was worn out with carrying sounds so long" (*Sound and Fury*, 140). Quentin clearly connects sound with the world of flux and experience. When Quentin questions Caddy at the branch about Dalton Ames, she apparently gives in to him, saying, "yes Ill do anything you want me to do anything yes" (194). Quentin's response tells everything about the panic her words generate: "you shut up." Caddy's words threaten to violate the ideal, to destroy his Eden, even though one part of Quentin knows that her liaison with Dalton Ames has already done the irrevocable damage. Still Quentin wants to wrap himself, and Caddy, in silence. The one way he can do this is by keeping his thoughts private.

One of Quentin's few successful attempts occurs when he thinks of Gerald Bland rowing:

> I could hear my watch and the train dying away, as though it were running through another month or another summer somewhere; rushing away under the poised gull and all things rushing. Except Gerald. He would be sort of grand too, pulling in a lonely state across the noon, rowing himself right out of noon, up the long bright air like an apotheosis, mounting into a drowsing infinity where only he and the gull, the one terrifically motionless, the other in a steady and measured pull and recover that partook of inertia itself, the world punily beneath their shadows on the sun. (*Sound and Fury*, 149)

Sound, which reminds him of time and movement, falls away as his imagination and language work together to turn action into stasis. The result lifts Gerald out of time and place until he *is* Quentin's glorified ideal. He wants to achieve the same apotheosis with Caddy. The Harvard chimes remind him:

> The first note sounded, measured and tranquil, serenely peremptory, emptying the unhurried silence for the next one and that's it if people could only change one another forever that way like a flame swirling up for an instant then blown cleanly out along the cool eternal dark instead of lying there trying not to think of the swing until all cedars came to have that vivid dead smell of perfume that Benjy hated so. (*Sound and Fury*, 219)

Quentin's tragedy is that someone's voice or chimes or a watch's ticking always breaks the silence.

But he is aware that even silence can be deceptive. He observes one of the three boys he has been watching subdue the other two by not answering their taunts: "they too partake of that adult trait of being convinced of anything by an assumption of silent superiority. I suppose that people, using themselves and each other so much by words, are at least consistent in attributing wisdom to a still tongue" (*Sound and Fury*, 146). Although the boy does show that silence can be a powerful communicator, and that language may bespeak nonsense and untruth, Quentin's scorn comes from firsthand experience that a still tongue does not connote wisdom. And that becomes his final terror.

Quentin knows that the only lasting silence comes in death. He has listened all his life. He knows the power words have, and yet he can never create with them the permanent, invulnerable perfection he seeks. Permanent silence is nothingness. We see that Quentin is moving toward death all along, but he also resists his passage by trying to make meaning. Finally he gives that up, but he still leaves the letters behind to put the remains of his life in order.[14]

Quentin Compson hates the paradox of language that he lives in. He believes it is power and he believes it is nothing. He knows it is inseparable from its context, and he fears the power of context to alter his words. He seeks a way out by continuing the debate and trying to create ideal, silent spaces of thought inside his own head. In *Absalom, Absalom!* he participates completely in the creation of the story of one man that grows into his own story.

Finally, in *The Sound and the Fury*, we witness the disintegration of his ability to live in the paradox.

The Sound and the Fury

The death of Quentin Compson does not mean the death of Faulkner's doubts about language, particularly since he resurrects Quentin several years later in *Absalom, Absalom!* But it does mark the realization of Faulkner's powers as a writer. Quentin is the dark extreme of his author's continuing debate about language; Quentin's desire for the absolute word begins to give way to Faulkner's discovery of the power in the interaction among many voices. Many of Quentin's fears continue to haunt Faulkner's work, but beginning with *The Sound and the Fury*, other voices compete. We can read Quentin's sense of loss, his fear of failure, in the rest of the novel, however.

We know that the novel began with an image, "the muddy seat of Caddy's drawers," and that Faulkner said he wrote each section because the previous one "failed."[15] The best criticism of the novel begins with the idea that Faulkner himself articulates, retrospectively assigning himself motives he could not have had at the actual writing: "I was trying to manufacture the sister which I did not have and the daughter which I was to lose" (Faulkner, "Introduction," 25). Loss and the attempt to recapture the lost permeates *The Sound and the Fury*.[16] Faulkner's self-acknowledged desire to retrieve Caddy through words must inform any discussion of the novel, but on another level, the novel is not about the loss of Caddy at all. André Bleikasten argues convincingly that she functions as the muse for all four narrators. The power that Faulkner has in creating her is as significant as the characters' inability to retrieve her. The novel also talks about the relationship between language and human consciousness—not just as an attempt to retrieve a loss, but as an exploration of the process of articulating thoughts and feelings into words. *The Sound and the Fury* avoids absolute meaning and repeats a story whose resolution remains elusive, but it also shows the successful articulation of four minds and their relationships to the language that gives them form. In each section, Faulkner explores a particular connection between the mind and language; each reveals an aspect of the power in language. That power is born out of the relation of language to consciousness. Faulkner begins by dramatizing the most elemental link between humans and language.

When Benjy Compson opens the gate to reach out to the little girl walking by, the nightmare of wordlessness becomes real: "I was trying to say, and I caught her, trying to say, and she screamed and I was trying to say and trying and the bright shapes began to stop and I tried to get out" (64). Benjy's need for Caddy merges with the trauma of inarticulateness, and here Benjy himself seems to understand the measure of his imprisonment. T. P. names the nature of Benjy's crisis when he tells him, " 'You cant do no good, moaning and slobbering through the fence' " (63). Without language Benjy cannot act; much of the world is closed to him.[17]

Through Benjy's words, which we come to understand are not his own, Faulkner carries us as far as is possible into the primitive, prelinguistic mind. The narrative of an idiot who can only bellow and moan to make himself known makes some of the most difficult and powerful reading in American literature. Words must be the medium, and Faulkner creates a mind that cannot understand the words that convey its reality. We come to understand Benjy from what other people say and from translating his thoughts into a wider, shared frame of reference. For example, when Benjy tells us that "a long piece of wire came across my shoulder. It went to the door, and then the fire went away" (70), we must figure from the context that Luster is teasing him by playing with the stove door. But Benjy Compson could not say even this, and the unreality of his words focuses attention on the word as necessary medium. That Benjy could never really narrate his section is exactly the point. Words cannot produce Benjy's actual state; instead, they mediate between us and the imagined but nevertheless real state that Faulkner seeks to create. The language in this section serves a conscious function as the ordering device, the translator of an otherwise incomprehensible mind. And of course it assumes an intelligent origin; Faulkner cannot avoid asserting the power that the narrator has by functioning as Benjy's spokesperson.

Benjy's love for Caddy stems from his dependence on her to

understand him. While she is with him, she translates his noise into sentences that we in turn need to understand him. When Caddy discovers that her perfume is the cause of Benjy's distress, she also voices his larger problem: "you are trying to tell Caddy and you couldn't tell her. You wanted to, but you couldn't" (51). After she articulates his concern, she takes Benjy and the perfume to Dilsey. In giving away the perfume, Caddy makes the necessary connection for Benjy between words and actions. At this point, she can remove physically the object of his distress and also facilitate our comprehension. Through Caddy, we connect the perfume with the crisis that her loss of sexual innocence creates, and thus a major thematic concern. But the scene also reveals that her sexual being only threatens Benjy because his need for her is so basic. She is his voice, his narrator, and her sexual experience will take her away from him.

Although Luster and T. P. talk to Benjy, and Dilsey loves him, only Caddy communicates *with* Benjy. Caddy defends his name change; she translates his moans for others and even instructs their mother on how to deal with him. The nature of their bond defines Benjy's loss in terms of his inability to say. Without language, Benjy is at the mercy of those around him. They react to his moaning, but no one after Caddy attempts to understand and to translate his sounds. Without language, Benjy's cries appear to others as "slow bellowing sound, meaningless" (356). One of the cruelest examples of Benjy's victimization occurs when Jason has him castrated after the incident at the gate. The tragedy of inarticulateness is that Benjy is alone, imprisoned. But clearly we are to feel the pain of Benjy's state more than he, for all of it that he knows is an occasional longing for Caddy. The final sentence of the section reiterates the connection between Caddy and Benjy's speechlessness: "Then the dark began to go in smooth, bright shapes, like it always does, even when Caddy says that I have been asleep" (92). Benjy remains in the dark world of shapes and sounds, where sleep and waking are ill-defined states without Caddy to say for him.

After the pathos of Benjy's "trying to say" and Quentin's obsessive anxiety about putting himself into words, Jason Compson appears to have the control his brothers lack. Jason tells us about himself in clear, direct language, but in turn, his words relentlessly expose his narrow-minded, often paranoiac outlook. We learn about Jason primarily through dramatic irony, which of course asserts the author's power and depends upon the reader's complicity. In Jason, we find a man whose lack of self-knowledge and separation from people finds a perfect corollary in his own separation from language. But again, Jason's "saying" fails because he uses language like he uses people.[18] Like Mr. Compson's, Jason's language is primarily monologic. He thinks that saying something makes it true ("Once a bitch always a bitch" [223]). He speaks in the declarative, "sane" language of a man who knows the world. But Faulkner turns both of Jason's weapons against him; Quentin runs off with his money and Jason's own words blind him but no one else.

Like Benjy and Quentin, Jason's relation to language defines his character. A crafty and brazen liar himself, Jason has a deep suspicion of words: "I make it a rule never to keep a scrap of paper bearing a woman's hand, and I never write them at all" (240). Yet Jason's day revolves around the negotiation of the letters he has received. He must intercept Caddy's letter to Quentin and deal with Caddy's demands to him. For a man who refuses to expose himself to the dangers of writing anything down, he has an enormous disregard for the words of others. And the control that he maintains over the household comes from his ability to lie, bully, and martyr himself in front of a susceptible audience. Jason's own manipulation of language makes him a shrewd reader—at least of others like himself. He understands exactly the parasitic greed behind his uncle Maury's pompous prose. But Jason's reading of Maury Bascomb's letter also tells us how to read *him*. Maury shares certain of Jason's attitudes: "My business experience has taught me to be chary of committing anything of a confidential nature to any more concrete medium than speech" (278), but more important, they are both betrayed by an absolute faith in the power of their words. Maury's flowery, obsequious letter exposes his desperate conniving to Jason and to us. And in turn, Jason's reading of his uncle's letter serves as our model for reading him. Jason's words are just as hypocritical and self-serving as Maury's.

Yet Jason is not simply the despicable villain who is undone by his own greed. His separation from the language is not complete. The same man whose internal diatribes against Jews, blacks, and women reveal only his petty irrationality also knows something of the power language can have in defusing a too-painful situation. Jason's first, bitter words assault us by undercutting the intensity of the two preceding sections, but his speech accurately points to an important aspect of Faulkner's method.[19] Some of Faulkner's most brilliant writing goes into the characterization of Jason, much of which manifests itself in black humor and a sharp-edged irony. The section is full of superbly comic moments, but they do more than simply provide opportunities to laugh at Jason; at times his wit takes incisive jabs at the core of the situation Faulkner has depicted so seriously in the first two sections.

Jason manipulates language with a little more success than he manipulates people and money. Words bolster his conviction that he is justified in cheating his "Christian forebearing" mother, and Jason's oratorical swagger indicates his understanding that words are power. Much of the time Faulkner lets Jason's words convict him, as in this particular self-incriminating delivery: "If there's one thing that gets under my skin, it's a damn hypocrite. A man that thinks anything he dont know all about must be crooked" (285). The rich irony comes out of our recognition that we are in a world where the biggest hypocrite of all can deliver an accurate definition of the term without including himself. But Jason also delivers, with biting accuracy, a balancing view of the Compsons— and he does so out of a need to control the situation. His means is language.

Jason displays all the characteristics of Freud's aggressive wit; he is "closely related to the sadist . . . sharp, alert, cold, aggressive and hostile."[20] Jason also exhibits an acute awareness of the absurdity of his situation, albeit not of himself. Early in the section, Jason's irritation at Luster for not changing the tire on his car generates a resentful attack on Benjy:

> It's bad enough on Sundays, with that damn field full of people that haven't got a side show and six niggers to feed, knocking a damn oversize mothball around. He's going to keep on running up and down that fence bellowing every time they come in sight until first

thing I know they're going to begin charging me golf dues, then Mother and Dilsey'll have to get a couple of china door knobs and a walking stick and work it out, unless I play at night with a lantern. Then they'd send us all to Jackson, maybe. God knows, they'd hold Old Home week when that happened. (232)

Anger expands the tirade against Benjy into a full-blown obsession about the general lunacy of his world. The images he creates are funny because they are irreverent. Yet they are also accurate. Jason's black humor combines the morbid and the absurd to offer a respite from the emotional intensity that has built up and then climaxed in Quentin's suicide. Our laughter becomes a valid human response because although we sympathize with Benjy, Jason's description of him sleeping, "the Great American Gelding snoring away like a planing mill" (328), delivers the sad reality of his world in a flash of brilliance. Because Jason is responsible for Benjy's castration, the horror of his words doubles the absurdity. Still there is humor when Jason calls Benjy the state asylum's "star freshman" (286) because from Jason's perspective he *is*, and laughter releases our pain.

By ridiculing Benjy and the Compson lineage, Jason assumes a superficial control over the situation. Language offers Jason power, while it offers Faulkner the greater means to strip Jason of any real control. But Jason's wit also comments upon the novel's efforts to articulate the Compson story. The most significant effect of his wit, once we acknowledge its paradoxical accuracy, is to refuse our greater sympathies for giving Benjy and Quentin any more authority. In the midst of real tragedy, we uncover a grotesque joke. Wit makes Jason both the object of laughter and the means through which we perceive how all the Compsons' inverted desires and twisted perceptions are both absurd and absolutely real. Faulkner knew well the value of a joke, for in Jason's final ruminations on Benjy's castration, there is the intimation that the author himself needed to undercut briefly his method: "And if they'd just sent him on to Jackson while he was under the ether, he'd never have known the difference. But that would have been too simple for a Compson to think of. Not half complex enough" (328–29). The first two sections of *The Sound and the Fury* attest to the accuracy of the last two statements, yet the joke in no way undermines their effect. Instead the humor clarifies the tragedy by grounding it in another layer of reality. Jason's version adds another dimension to an already complex story even as it mocks its own method. Humor also underscores the absurdity of a world so terrible that the brutal sharpness of Jason's wit allows us a momentary relief from the complexity.

But Faulkner does not allow the absurdity that Jason uncovers to stand as an ultimate meaning. Rather, to refuse Jason the last word, Faulkner presents the fourth, and omniscient, narrator whose ostensible objectivity offers yet another perspective. The section's very existence makes all of the sections a series of interpretations rather than a cumulative progression toward meaning; we find no answers in section 4, only another way of reading the Compson story.[21]

By keeping us outside a single character's consciousness this time, Faulkner underscores the idea that he has been developing all along—meaning resides in the exchanges among a community of narrators and readers. Section 4 is another test of literary discourse, to borrow from Bakhtin. His theory of the novel's essential heteroglossia is particularly helpful in reading *The Sound and the Fury* because it centers on the relational and contextual aspects of making meaning. In "Discourse in the Novel," Bakhtin distinguishes the novel from other genres in terms of the exchange that Faulkner emphasizes by writing the novel in sections: "The language of the novel becomes an artistically organized system of languages. . . . a language is revealed in all its distinctiveness only when it is brought into relationship with other languages, entering with them into one single heteroglot unit of societal becoming" (410–11). For Faulkner, both the idea of language as intrinsically social and his view of himself as the creator of language are problematic. But the tension between them also fuels his writing. Section 4 contains a remarkable scene that illustrates precisely the idea that the interaction among languages, with their potential to condition and to revise, makes meaning.

The illuminating effect of Reverend Shegog's sermon on Dilsey and the others in the congregation comes out of the process by which he gives it. The sermon is the retelling of an old story, a celebration of the memory of suffering and salvation translated into a familiar tongue: " 'I got de ricklickshun en de blood of de Lamb!' " (368). The sermon is also the story of a man who becomes his voice and, in the becoming, touches others. Shegog speaks the language of his audience and he delivers the Word, which passes "beyond the need for words" (367). Shegog transforms the Word of God, the ultimate authoritative discourse, into words his congregation then makes its own. Some critics see this as Faulkner's endorsement of and struggle toward a communication more perfect than words, but although Dilsey undergoes enlightenment, her vision is private.[22] In addition, Shegog's words ignite wordless communication among kindred hearts *because* the words are familiar. Finally the sermon itself is a medium between the congregation and its collective experience and identification with the Easter myth. Words are unnecessary only because everyone knows them already. And it is through the telling of the sermon that Dilsey can place the Compson story in perspective: " 'I've seed de first en de last' " (371). Shegog's language has its greatest meaning when it is "brought into relationship" with Dilsey's. The sermon helps Dilsey place the present into context—"seeing" the Compson history orders the nevertheless devastated present. Similarly, the fourth section is another language brought into the widening context of the novel.

It is also true that although Dilsey can make a meaningful connection to Christ's suffering and the end of the Compson's, that connection is not necessarily the reader's, nor does her understanding allow her to change anything. Shegog's sermon does tell of the power that words possess, but only when they articulate a common memory. Inherent in the power that words have is the suggestion that they cannot affect anyone for whom the words are foreign. Shegog could never reach Jason or explain Benjy except in terms of Christ's suffering. The experiental nature of language is an implicit subject of *The Sound and the Fury*, as Faulkner explores the links between consciousness and language in the context of so many failed communications. The human instinct is to articulate the self, but again and again we see articulation is fumbled or choked off from an audience within the novel. For reasons as different as they are, none of the Compson brothers can communicate effectively. Language remains an interior tool for them, and the effort is to articulate consciousness, not to seek solutions or to establish connections with other people.

The descriptions of both Benjy and Jason in section 4 tend to support the limited powers of language. Benjy's cries are "hopeless and prolonged . . . nothing. Just sound. It might have been all time and injustice and sorrow become vocal for an instant by a conjunction of planets" (359). The description both denies meaning and suggests it. If Benjy's cries are "hopeless" and do embody "all time and injustice and sorrow," they do so for the narrator and for the reader, but not for Benjy. We know from section 1 that Benjy's responses are much more immediate and concrete than the kind of protest against fate that the narrator describes. The play of meaning, then, exists beyond the original consciousness. The narrator repeatedly exhibits the impulse to make meaning; another time he links Benjy's cries to "all voiceless misery under the sun" (395). But the narrator also underscores the conditional nature of interpretation in the verb phrase "might have been," from the first quotation, and the suggestion that Benjy's articulation of universal pain occurs because of some planetary accident furthers the notion that meaning is neither fixed nor absolute.

The narrator also describes Jason in terms of the failure of his language. When he tells the sheriff about Quentin's escape with "his" money, the narrator describes the telling as "his sense of injury and impotence feeding upon its own sound, so that after a time he forgot his haste in the violent cumulation of his self justification and his outrage" (378). Through this description, we learn that we have read Jason correctly—or that Jason has told himself well. The description is also evidence of Faulkner's impulse to tell again and to connect Jason to a wider realm of meaning. Jason's impotence feeds upon "its own sound"—the words remind us of Benjy, whose cries are "just sound." And both descriptions bring to mind the novel's title, which in turn alludes to Macbeth's bleak assessment of human endeavor. As a novel that so worries over the endeavor of putting experience into words, *The Sound and the Fury*'s title again questions its own authority. The allusion enriches our reading of the novel, but neither Shakespeare nor Faulkner believe they tell a tale "signifying nothing." Jason's words mean nothing that he wants them to mean, but the narrator's description of Jason does reiterate the one he unwittingly gives us: Jason is unable to make meaning, in this case, because of his own twisted self-perception. But the narrator also alludes to another level of meaning that opens the possibilities for interpretation. The intertextual weaving of *Macbeth* and the whole Christian Easter myth into the novel speak not to the failure of language but to its capacity to sustain the experience. *The Sound and the Fury* is about a dying family; it returns obsessively to the loss of Caddy, whose name is the logographic center of her brothers' anguish. But in this novel, Faulkner finds his way out of the sense of loss that he assigns a killing power in Quentin's section.

The story continues for Faulkner, as the appendix affirms. Once more he relates it by delineating the Compson history. As Shegog's sermon shows Dilsey, Faulkner again tells us that in setting out the past, we can explain the present. But to counteract any impulse to latch onto an ultimate meaning, Faulkner keeps his tone speculative when he is not relating the facts of each person's life. He also tells us nothing new about the characters in the novel; he simply puts them into other words and tells what happens to them after the novel ends. Most important, he arranges the appendix chronologically and thus suggests its pertinence to the story, but he makes no other attempt to connect any of the descriptions. The sequence invites interpretation but does not itself interpret. The appendix does not explicitly answer anything, except that it illustrates again Faulkner's belief that the valuable endeavor is the process of telling. The conclusion is less significant because avoiding the absolute resolution keeps language alive to possibilities.

In "Another Version" of the preface to *The Sound and the Fury*, Faulkner comments on the value of telling, particularly for the Southerner: "We need to talk, to tell, since oratory is our heritage. . . . I have tried to escape (the South) and I have tried to indict. After five years, I look back at *The Sound and the Fury* and see that that was the turning point: in this book I did both at one time" ("An Introduction," 25). Faulkner's admission of his Quentin-like desire to escape the South and his recognition of the South's presence in his writing points to his growing respect for the other—the voices of the past and of the present—in his writing. That Faulkner wrote not one but two introductions also speaks to the deliberately unfinished nature of this novel. Faulkner seems always to have more to say. Then also, he speaks of his own personal and conflicting reasons for writing, these in addition to his more familiar desire to create his own little girl. With this novel, Faulkner affirms the powers of language to express the self and even to realize an object of desire. But he also creates a novel that cultivates an exchange between narrator and reader that is separate from the meaning the narrative has for its creator. In doing so, Faulkner defines writing as the result of two conflicting impulses: "I had made myself a vase, but I suppose I knew all the time that I could not live forever inside of it" ("An Introduction," 27). The exchange between word and mind keeps the word alive, but that same exchange also threatens to alter the word. In *The Sound and the Fury*, Faulkner moves beyond his implicit desire in writing *Flags in the Dust;* here he creates his vase and allows for its continual reworking.

Absalom, Absalom!

By the time Faulkner wrote *Absalom*, he had seemingly given up the notion of creating the immutable word, his perfect vase. Indeed the novel evolves from the premise that language creates reality through interplay between the creating mind (the teller) and the receiving mind (the listener/reader). Yet Faulkner does still worry about the overarching problem with granting these particular powers to language—that reality is then made subjective, speculative, and vulnerable to change. For example, as Mr. Compson tells Quentin about Judith Sutpen and Charles Bon, he digresses to contemplate the fundamental difficulty facing all readers—how to know what the words mean:

And your grandfather said, "Suffer little children to come unto Me" and what did He mean by that? how, if He meant that little children should need to *be* suffered to approach Him, what sort of earth had He created; that if they had to suffer in order to approach Him, what sort of Heaven did He have? (248)

Quentin's grandfather identifies the reader's desire to look beyond an author's often ambiguous words to the higher authority of the author himself. The separation of author from word, particularly when the Word is God, underscores the potential ambiguity of all language and involves the reader in the process of giving meaning to words. *Absalom, Absalom!* repeatedly confronts its characters and its readers with the question of how to know the meaning of its words. But rather than becoming trapped in ambiguity, *Absalom* seeks to pass through it and to map out a workable means of communication between teller and listener or reader. The elder Compson's questions open the text to the reader as they define the text's limitations. Exegesis is also, of course, an exercise of power equal to writing.

For all the ways in which Faulkner explores the intricacies of narration—of making and communicating meaning—in this novel, he still works to assert the power of his word. He is acutely aware that every declaration he makes for the power of language must also acknowledge its imprecision. Of all the novels, *Absalom* maintains most brilliantly the balance between the powers and hazards in our relation to language. As Faulkner's most complete and most complex investigation into the subject of narration, *Absalom* has proved to be fertile ground for the recent critical interest in language theory and reader engagement in the text. My conviction that the novel defines and ultimately celebrates the power of language and literature is both informed by and often in opposition to those commentators who read *Absalom* as a self-reflexive text.[23] The prevailing critical stance is that Faulkner's investigation of narrative art ends in the recognition that language can never truly reconstitute action or experience. I find, however, that Faulkner declares the ultimate power of his novel to create provocative and productive exchanges between itself and its readers. And though

Absalom does insist upon the primacy of invention and exchange among many narrators, the novel still asserts the power of its one author.

For all the variation in tone and perspective in the different narrations, the language of *Absalom* unites all disparate elements in an overarching sameness. Noting Faulkner's own description of the language of *Absalom* as "oratory out of solitude," Stephen Ross writes persuasively of the connections between Southern oratory, essentially a monologic discourse, and Bakhtin's concept of the dialogical in the novel. Ross argues that the rhetorical habits of the novel's several voices merge into an "overvoice" that threatens but finally enriches its polyphony.[24] *Absalom* does, of course, take the idea of narrative as dialogic for its very subject, but the novel's language also asserts an authorial presence that puts narrative authority at issue. When Quentin observes that Shreve sounds just like his father and then that "maybe we are both Father" (326), he gives voice to the seriousness of this struggle to overcome and to become the authority. Ross also notes that all the narrators "sound like father," but I want to focus on the issue of authority in authoring for what it reveals of Faulkner's own desire toward monologue. The language of *Absalom* asserts an authorial presence that allows for a character's individuality but never gives way to it. All of the narrators compose long, dense sentences that consider all possibilities and attempt to omit no detail. They share metaphors and implicitly, a faith in and dependence upon language. They all sound like Faulkner. To clarify this statement and to distinguish between the author and narrator, I turn again to "Discourse in the Novel." Bakhtin reminds us that the author is behind but not in the narrator. The author negotiates among languages and thus asserts a freedom and power greater than any narrator. Faulkner writes his exploration of that power into *Absalom*. Bakhtin further argues that stylistics separated from genre study isolates language from its actual, social context. In calling *Absalom* cursed by both his own solitude and Southern oratory, Faulkner concurs and uncovers the paradox of a language born out of isolation *and* a particular region. Bakhtin speaks of the style of a novel as a "higher unity" composed of "the system of its languages" ("Discourse in the Novel," 262), and it is that effort toward a higher unity that becomes for Faulkner an issue of his own authority.

To illustrate the presence in *Absalom* that controls our perception of the book as a coherent and regulated system of signs, I refer to the opening pages. The narrator describes the scent of "twice-bloomed wistaria against the outer wall by the savage quiet September sun impacted distilled and hyperdistilled" (4). Four chapters later, the same wistaria reminds Rosa of her fourteenth summer, and she asks Quentin, " 'Do you mark how the wistaria, sun-impacted on this wall here, distills and penetrates this room as though (light-unimpeded) by secret and attritive progress from mote to mote of obscurity's myriad components?' " (178). Rosa's observation is somewhat more ornate, but the similarities in the two descriptions are unmistakable. Neither sounds like spoken language. A common vocabulary is the most concrete connection between the two, but there is also a shared sense of luxuriating in language. Both narrators work their words, forming compounds and complicating the syntax. Both narrators invest the scent of wistaria with significance, creating out of it a symbol of a dusty, faded past that is not really past at all. To solidify further the connections they make, when Quentin, now at Harvard, receives his father's letter in chapter 7, "that dead summer twilight—the wistaria . . . attenuate[s] up from Mississippi" (217).[25] Although distance apparently weakens the strength of the memory, the simple mention of wistaria weights it with meaning and links it again to the past.

The authorial presence is particularly significant in a novel that insists upon the necessity for invention and open-ended exchange. The two notions are not antithetical, however. To read *Absalom, Absalom!* is to experience language as a real force. The words spill over the pages, accumulating power not only in terms of their number, but through their figurative potential as well.[26] As the different narrators tell their stories, they partake of the same faith that characterizes the premise of the entire novel: words are all that we have to articulate reality and *more* words will refine and clarify previous articulation. The stylistic unit that *Absalom* attains holds together the five narrative voices, even as they revise and erase one another. We see separate, private dramas enacted through the processes of narration, giving no one narrator authority over more than his subjective narrative. But each does establish control through the creation of his narrative—for a time at least. The continual presence of another, whose existence always threatens revision, exerts its most telling pressure on Mr. Compson's words. Ultimately, Faulkner tells us that Quentin's father is wrong to believe that meaning is static and resides inside the "shadowy inscrutable" word.[27] Mr. Compson's insistence upon the disjunction between word and referent minimizes the power of words to activate imagination and continually frustrates his own admitted desire to know what the words mean.

Mr. Compson's approach to the Sutpen story is limiting and serves as another means by which Faulkner can highlight the very real barriers to effective articulation and exchange. Faulkner grants Mr. Compson the undeniable fact that words are symbols and therefore mere representations. But instead of viewing that truth as a limitation, Faulkner handicaps Mr. Compson, who cannot see that negotiating the symbolic nature of words is the paradigm for all human endeavor. Mr. Compson's blindness to the symbolism inherent in all action traps him in his perception of language's inadequacy. In *Absalom*, the facts that Henry Sutpen murders Charles Bon and that Wash Jones kills Thomas Sutpen prove to be no less symbolic or subject to inference than the letter that Judith gives to Quentin's grandmother. The acts are simply the known centers from which the narrators invent, speculate, and infer. Unlike Mr. Compson's effort to emphasize the insignificance of Bon's letter, the novel asserts the plenitude of significance in every known or supposed incident.

Factual evidence of past events is slight—a few crumbling letters "without salutation or signature, in which men and women who once lived and breathed are now merely initials or nicknames" (124); the cryptic words on intended gravestones; and of course, Quentin's climactic discovery of Henry Sutpen. In each case, a few, unembellished words connect an experience in the past to the present. The meeting with Henry provides Quentin with the experience, and thus the authority that his father lacks. In his sparse, palindromic exchange with Henry, Quentin confronts the flesh and blood referent of his words:

> *And you are—?*
> *Henry Sutpen.*
> *And you have been here—?*
> *Four years.*
> *And you came home—?*
> *To die. Yes.*
> *To die.*
> *Yes. To die.*
> *And you have been here—?*
> *Four years.*
> *And you are—?*
> *Henry Sutpen.* (464–65)

Although stripped of the novel's characteristically discursive style, the words create their own suspended drama. For a moment, the reality of Henry Sutpen erases the need for the many words that have gone into reconstructing his actions and supposing his motives. The language communicates simply what is necessary. The stark recitation of facts occurs one other time in the novel, when the narrator recreates a pivotal scene between Henry and Judith:

> *Now you cant marry him.*
> *Why cant I marry him?*
> *Because he's dead.*
> *Dead?*
> *Yes. I killed him.* (215)

Again words that are almost brutal in their simplicity convey the crucial information. The telling of the significant action is again more important than the recreation of that action. In fact, in this exchange, words actually become action, as Judith and Henry stand "speaking to one another in short brief staccato sentences like slaps."[28] The incident asserts articulation as the crucial action of the novel; all of the material evidence for Sutpen's life story appears as simple, yet troublesome words.

The sparse exchanges in each of these two passages place us

immediately at the center of Faulkner's dialectic of language. In both cases we confront the knowledge that, as Mr. Compson says, all that we and the characters have are "just the words, the symbols, the shapes themselves, shadowy inscrutable and serene, against the turgid background of a horrible and bloody mischancing of human affairs" (125). Only a few stark words represent crucial, past acts. Yet the novel consistently works to overcome the inadequacies of language as the medium between past and present, thought and deed, and teller and listener. And Faulkner accomplishes this through the sheer force of his words. From the first labyrinthine sentence, we are coaxed inside a "still hot weary dead" world into which only words breathe life. *Absalom* is the first of Faulkner's great novels to be written entirely in the dense, complicated prose that is most often thought of as the Faulknerian style. Except for the few staccato exchanges mentioned above, *Absalom* is constructed almost entirely out of very long, convoluted sentences. In *Faulkner in the University*, Faulkner describes the rationale behind his style in terms particularly appropriate for this novel: "A character in a story at any moment of action is not just himself as he is then, he is all that made him, and the long sentence is an attempt to get his past and possibly his future into the instant in which he does something."[29] As Gary Stonum has noted, Faulkner's style does afford him with the means to take personal possession of both the past and of his material.[30] But the Faulknerian sentence manifests an even more subtle kind of control. Like Quentin, Faulkner also invests in language the power to say everything. If we in the present are the sum of our past experiences and future possibilities, then Faulkner asks nothing less of his words than that they say so.

Aside from the fact that the subject of the novel is the narrative process, *Absalom, Absalom!* celebrates the sheer force of language. The book's five narrators often struggle to construct their narratives. Their difficulties and even failures never stop the flow of words; each narrator tries to say it all, within the limits of his or her own imagination. Details fill the pages, and sentences swell with alternative possibilities and extended speculations. From the beginning, language engulfs the reader as it does Quentin. Rosa

Coldfield begins to talk about the ghost-filled past, and the narrator's sentences expand and grow denser:

> Her voice would not cease, it would just vanish. There would be the dim coffin-smelling gloom sweet and oversweet with the twice-bloomed wistaria against the outer wall by the savage quiet September sun impacted distilled and hyperdistilled, into which came now and then the loud cloudy flutter of the sparrows like a flat limber stick whipped by an idle boy, and the rank smell of female old flesh long embattled in virginity while the wan haggard face watched him above the faint triangle of lace at wrists and throat from the too tall chair in which she resembled a crucified child; and the voice not ceasing but vanishing into and then out of the long intervals like a stream, a trickle running from patch to patch of dried sand, and the ghost mused with shadowy docility as if it were the voice which he haunted where a more fortunate one would have had a house. (4)

The two sentences appear to meander with the same flowing aimlessness as Rosa's voice. Rather than giving the sense of progress toward a single point, the second sentence stops to expand and reinforce the first. Meaning unfolds and grows richer as the words accumulate. Synesthesia attempts to encompass varied sensory effects, oxymoron gathers together contradiction, and multiple adjectives detail the moment. To reinforce an atmosphere filled with ghosts too long suppressed, words are repeated and compounded, packing the sentence tight with meaning. We are meant to linger over the effects of these words, not to consume them in a rush to the end. Faulkner means to immerse us in language; that in itself is an assertion of authorial control. Faulkner avoids what Bakhtin calls "monological discourse" as much through sentences and paragraphs and chapters that seek to tell everything as by his several narrators.

Just as Quentin Compson's fears about language counterbalance Faulkner's assertions of its power in *Absalom*, as well as in *The Sound and the Fury*, the writing itself embodies dialogue about the power of the word. One particularly Faulknerian habit illustrates this well: the parenthesis. As a syntactical device, parentheses contain necessary, additional information. Faulkner's parenthetical expressions often carry more than just information about the narrative; they also comment directly upon the act of writing.

I return to a passage from *Absalom* that comments in several ways about narration:

> It (the talking, the telling) seemed (to him, to Quentin) to partake of the logic- and reason-flouting quality of a dream which the sleeper knows must have occurred, stillborn and complete, in a second, yet the very quality upon which it must depend to move the dreamer (verisimilitude) to credulity—horror or pleasure or amazement—depends as completely upon a formal recognition of and acceptance of elapsed and yet-elapsing time as music or a printed tale. (22–23)

The first two sets of parentheses are particularly interesting because they are so clearly *about* the anxiety over the word's ability to be precise. Their presence can be justified in no other way, for if clarity were the motive, the sentence would simply begin, "The telling seemed to Quentin." The parentheses seem to exist solely to call attention to the act of revising toward greater precision. Achieving precision through language becomes the issue. And finally, the parentheses say that such precision is possible. By *not* placing *(verisimilitude)* next to the word it modifies, *quality*, but next to *dreamer*, the narrator also asserts his control. By flouting a rule of English grammar, he keeps language open to possibility and to the will of its user. Thus in a passage whose subject is the power of fiction upon its audience, we find the narrator's subtle demonstration of the power words give their users. Faulkner makes the same comment every time he disregards common punctuation rules such as the comma to separate items in a series or the apostrophe in contractions such as *dont*.

If the authorial voice says anything, it speaks to the power of language to articulate memory and imagination. But while strongly asserting the order and control inherent in language, Faulkner constantly reminds us that the order is subjective and the control temporary. But above all else, *Absalom, Absalom!* asserts the necessity of fiction-making and its constant possibility for saying it all. Faulkner's own comments on the varied perspectives in *Absalom* voice his paradoxical outline for learning what the words mean:

> Taken all together, the truth is in what they saw though nobody saw the truth intact. So these [perspectives] are true as far as Miss

Rosa and Quentin saw it. . . . But the truth, I would like to think, comes out, that when the reader has read all these thirteen different ways of looking at the blackbird, the reader has his own fourteenth image of that blackbird which I would like to think is the truth.[31]

By acknowledging the limitations of each of his narrators, Faulkner admits to the subjectivity and relativity of language. But by granting the reader the greater powers of perception, Faulkner endorses the novel as an entity that does contain truths. Even that assertion of a central, fixed "truth" is qualified in the implicit recognition that the novel's every reader will revise the truth. *Absalom*'s greatest power is that it makes a definitive statement about the viability of language while it remains unfinished and open to possibility.

3

As I Lay Dying
and *Light in August:*
Communities of Language

> I enter the hall, hearing the voices before I reach the door.
> . . . As you enter the hall, they sound as though they were
> speaking out of the air about your head.—Darl Bundren in
> *As I Lay Dying*

> He was hearing a myriad sounds of no greater volume—
> voices, murmurs, whispers: of trees, darkness, earth;
> people: his own voice; other voices evocative of names and
> times and places—which he had been conscious of all his life
> without knowing it, which were his life.—*Light in August*

As I Lay Dying (1930) and *Light in August* (1932) contemplate multivoiced worlds without the sense of morbid threat that fills the novels of Horace Benbow and Quentin Compson. Certainly in both, Faulkner reminds us that words can trap and deceive, but he also writes with an easier acceptance of language as dialogue. Although Faulkner has said that both novels were less inspired than deliberate and that by the time of their writing he "had learned too much about his trade," his jadedness belies the novels' power.[1] They share more than the fact that they were written within two years of each other. Both reveal Faulkner's determined exploration of the ways that the words of others intersect with his own. Although death is at the center of both, and *Light in August* is saturated with the grim violence of racism and misogyny, the novels mark Faulkner's fullest development of our communal ties to language.

As he did in *The Sound and the Fury*, Faulkner investigates connections between language and consciousness in *As I Lay Dying*, and he also relies on multiple perspectives to tell a story without an authoritative version. The voices of Addie and Darl Bundren warn against belief in the absolute power of words, and in *Light in August*, the lives of Joe Christmas and Joanna Burden are destroyed by rigid definitions of the word *Negro*. That novel also introduces Gavin Stevens, Faulkner's man of words matured, and the successfully socialized mouthpiece for the racist theory of blood. But *As I Lay Dying* comes closer than *The Sound and the Fury* to validating the ordering power of language that is shot through with the presence of others. The exchange of narrative responsibility between Darl and Cash Bundren allows Faulkner to assess the nature of a narrator's, and by extension a writer's, powers. The single, anonymous narrator of *Light in August* grasps those powers to make public what is to a much greater extent in *As I Lay Dying* the articulation of the private self. Yet again Faulkner weaves into both texts a dialogue that challenges the powers of language. The most outright challenge comes in *As I Lay Dying*.

As I Lay Dying

Although Addie Bundren's famous indictment of words comes nearly two-thirds of the way into the novel, Faulkner has been arguing with her from the first page.[2] Addie is the novel's most emphatic speaker against belief in the efficacy of language; her voice is clear and persuasive because experience has taught her that there is no debate—"words dont ever fit even when they are trying to sat at."[3] She has formidable support in the manipulative Anse and in the self-serving, rhetorically empty words of Reverend Whitfield and Cora Tull, but her denouncement of language is finally less significant than the fact that she talks about language at all.[4] Addie states outright just one side of the dialogue about language that Faulkner makes the subtext of this polyphonic novel. While Addie is the novel's strongest proponent of the frailty of language, Darl Bundren embodies the conviction that the word can create reality and connect isolated consciousnesses. In the opening paragraph, his detailed physical description of Jewel and him walking on the path exhibits what we soon see is a strong faith that language makes memory, perception, and action real.[5] And as the novel's most frequent speaker, he displays the omniscience, verbal range, and responsibility for interpretation that we associate with a narrator.

On the other hand, Anse and Cora's sections act as the prelude to Addie's section, which is situated far enough into the novel so that we have also seen the tortuous convolutions of Darl's own consciousness. In spite of his growing unreliability, Darl aids our realization that Addie has been isolated and deceived by what was once an absolute faith in words. The unbearable gap between word and deed has emptied her of feeling and the world of meaning. But Darl points out in an anticipatory rebuttal that deeds can be as empty as the words that name them: " 'The safe things are just the things that folks have been doing so long they have worn the edges off and there's nothing to the doing of them' " (117). When Addie talks with yearning of "the dark land talking the voiceless speech" (161), she articulates the seductive paradox of perfect communication in silence. But soon after, Darl reminds us that true silence means death: "How do our lives ravel out into the no-wind, no-sound, the weary gestures wearily recapitulant" (191). Faulkner complicates the dialogue by having Addie bind herself to her father's stultifying axiom—"the reason for living is getting ready to stay dead" (162)—and also by binding her family to her deathbed promise. But Darl's refutation is shaped in the brilliant rhetoric of madness. Between the dead and the mad, however, Faulkner establishes a range of possibilities for language. Central to the dialogue that Addie and Darl frame is the evolution of Cash as a reliable narrator.

Bakhtin's insistence in "Discourse in the Novel" that "the word does not exist in a neutral and impersonal language" (294) echoes throughout *As I Lay Dying*. Addie knows but refuses to accept this; Darl accepts it but pushes the play between word and deed/

speaker and listener too far. Only Cash grows to accommodate the other in language. The novel, according to Bakhtin, is the ultimate recognition of language as always contingent upon context and thus never absolute nor static. His theory offers a way to read the subtext of *As I Lay Dying*. The novel moves, always in the shadow of Addie's words, to seek connections among its fifteen separate narrators.

The very structure of *As I Lay Dying* indicates Faulkner's interest in articulating consciousness; the number of narrators provides him the means to explore how language connects these otherwise isolated narrators. Characteristically, Faulkner considers every possibility and limitation in language that his narrators suggest; the novel moves dialogically among them. To paraphrase Bakhtin, it presents perspectives and opposing evaluations to provide the interaction that will allow Faulkner to move freely among the words of his narrators ("Discourse in the Novel," 314). Anse Bundren, Cora Tull, and Reverend Whitfield are linked by their reliance on language to justify themselves. They all believe that saying something makes it true, and dramatic irony undermines them all. In the sections narrated by Peabody, Tull, Armstid, and the others outside the Bundren family, language links interior visions to the external world. The characters react to the Bundrens and thus connect their isolated, often obscure thoughts to a more public context. When Tull, for example, says that Darl looks at people "like he had got into the inside of you, some way" (*As I Lay Dying*, 111), he placed Darl's extraordinary perceptions into the ordinary world. Thoughts are real; Darl's words are not just private creations.

Faulkner also expands Addie Bundren's indictment of the word in Jewel's one section. Jewel's words are quick and clear and propelled by his anger. Like his mother, Jewel yearns for the peace of silence: "One lick less and we could be quiet" (14). He also acts out of apparently the same suspicion of words; Jewel's presence in the novel is consistently one of rigid but quick actions, almost completely formulated from the words of others. Cash's initial alienation from language changes as the novel progresses, but he consistently displays the belief in a rational correlation between thought and language and the external world. A variation of that belief comes from Dewey Dell who, because she is pregnant, makes continual connections between herself and the cycles of nature. She also separates herself from the males who surround her, particularly Darl. Her consciousness is an intensely private one that both hates its isolation and works to integrate itself into an apparently female life principle that exists beyond individuals and beyond words. She feels an affinity with the cow in the barn that she never feels for any person; Dewey Dell says she feels "like a wet seed wild in the hot blind earth" (58). The metaphor articulates Dewey Dell's kinship with a primitive, wordless life, but it also reaffirms her own higher ability to perceive and articulate the relationship.

It is through Vardaman and Darl, however, that Faulkner most carefully delineates the process of making perceptions understandable and thus real through language. Both characters expose the most basic relation between humans and words. Central to that relationship is the need and ability to make metaphor. Metaphor respects the gap between word and thing while it strives to close it. Faulkner's investigation of metaphor here reveals an essential aspect of his growth as a novelist. As I noted in chapter 1, Faulkner's description of himself as a "failed poet" is informed by his sense of the poet's greater power to name and preserve experience. Again according to Bakhtin, the metaphoric language of the novel is different from that of poetry because of prose's "double-voicedness" ("Discourse in the Novel," 328), or its recognition of the other's voice that will inevitably color or alter the author's intentions. Understanding metaphor also entails recognizing the relational nature of reality. Vardaman exists in the rudimentary stages of grasping the concept of metaphor. Continually he struggles to make himself real by articulating his relation to those around him. Similarly he tries to understand his mother's death in terms of the fish he kills: "Then it wasn't and she was, and now it is and she wasn't" (60). Vardaman sets up a causal relationship between Addie and the fish that leads to his ultimate conclusion: "My mother is a fish" (74). In that strange declaration, Vardaman realizes the abstraction of death through metaphor. Later how-

ever, we see that his child's mind cannot understand the sophisticated wordplay that Darl engages him in. When Darl tells him
that Jewel's mother is a horse, Vardaman quickly asserts that then
his mother is a fish. But he is still too literal to follow through—he
reasons finally, " 'Then mine will have to be a horse too' " (89).

Darl leads Vardaman into an extension of the word game that
allows Darl to hurt Jewel verbally and to spoof his own reliance
on the process of articulating the self. Vardaman begins the exchange by asking:

> "Then what is your ma, Darl?"
> "I haven't got ere one," Darl said. "Because if I had one, it is *was*.
> And if it is was, it can't be *is*. Can it?"
> "No," I said.
> "Then I am not," Darl said. "Am I?"
> "No," I said.
> I am. Darl is my brother.
> "But you *are* Darl," I said.
> "I know it," Darl said. "That's why I am not is. *Are* is too many
> for one woman to foal." (89–90)

Vardaman maintains his precarious hold on reality, or the way
things *are*, by voicing himself ("I am") and Darl ("Darl is my
brother"). Both he and Darl try to orient themselves by putting
ideas into words. Vardaman's struggles here make him the unwitting straight man in Darl's linguistic joke. Darl himself has en-
gaged in the sort of intellection that he turns into a game. The
process is usually syllogistic and attempts to make concrete the
abstractions of death and time: "The wagon *is*, because when the
wagon is *was*, Addie Bundren will not be. And Jewel *is*, so Addie
Bundren must be. And then I must be, or I could not empty myself
for sleep in a strange room. And so if I am not emptied yet, I
am *is*" (72). The falseness of Darl's syllogism is secondary to its
significance as the manifestation of the verbal nature of Darl's
mind. For him, the self and its relation to others exist when he
can put them into words. His exchange with Vardaman allows him
to flex his verbal muscles, and by making articulation a game, Darl
asserts his own control over the words that he so depends on.

Vardaman and Darl engage in the most overt attempt to connect themselves to other people and to make death real through language, but the comprehension of reality through metaphor is also a community endeavor. In *As I Lay Dying*, language is the connector among isolated perceptions. Noting that several narrators use the same metaphor to describe Cash's sawing, Stephen Ross asserts that language does not reveal consciousness but rather *is* consciousness.[6] Ross argues convincingly that individuality is a matter of expression rather than of perception. But these collective perceptions actually make language the only connection among these people. To have four different narrators liken Cash's sawing to snoring is to link all four perceptions through their language.

An even wider network of connections begins with Cora Tull's observation that Addie's eyes "are like two candles when you watch them gutter down into the sockets of iron candle-sticks" (7). Later Doc Peabody says that Addie's eyes "look like lamps blaring up just before the oil is gone" (41). Then Darl sees Addie's death in her eyes: "the two flames glare up for a steady instant. Then they go out as though someone had leaned down and blown upon them" (44). The common metaphor unifies and validates their perceptions. Further, the metaphor becomes the understood, concrete reality. But the language each uses to form the metaphor is also different, underscoring the relational nature of language, its dependence on the other. To the same effect, both Anse and Dewey Dell describe Darl's eyes as "full of the land" (32), and Tull, Armstid, and Darl compare Jewel's eyes to pieces of white china. Formulating perceptions into words makes meaning and gives them coherence. Because the metaphors are shared, they declare language as a possible link among otherwise isolated consciousnesses.

To strengthen the link, Faulkner gives Darl uncommon powers of omniscience. Darl describes Addie's death while he stands in the rain with Jewel, trying to repair a broken wagon wheel. When he imagines Dewey Dell's reaction to the death, he sees her obsessed with her pregnancy, saying to Doc Peabody in her thoughts, "You could do so much for me if you just would" (47). Just six pages later, Dewey Dell's section begins, "He could do so much for me if he just would." Darl knows his sister's mind well enough to know her exact words. *As I Lay Dying* shows language to be the assembler of thought, a window on the human mind, and wherever language is the same or similar, it acts as a bridge. But Darl's knowledge of Dewey Dell cannot break through their isolation, and perception of the dialogue between them is primarily the reader's because the words are articulations of thought. But Darl and Dewey Dell communicate nonetheless, apparently by reading each other's faces: "I saw Darl and he knew. He said he knew without the words like he told me that ma is going to die without words" (24). Dewey Dell hates Darl for his knowledge, and as the novel progresses, Darl's heightened awareness grows too acute for the ordinary world.

In spite of the novel's technique of multiple perspectives, Darl's language calls special attention to his capacity as narrator. That he is mad adds a significant complication to Faulkner's exploration of the narrative process. Out of the fifteen narrators who offer perspectives, Darl assumes much of the responsibility for setting forth scenes, for explaining events, and for articulating the thoughts of others. As a narrator who is aware of his role, Darl is also the most aware of language. When the wagon passes a sign announcing New Hope Church, Darl interprets the faded lettering:

> It wheels up like a motionless hand lifted above the profound desolation of the ocean; beyond it the red road lies like a spoke of which Addie Bundren is the rim. It wheels past, empty, underscored, the white signboard turns away its fading and tranquil assertion. (95)

At the same time that Darl associates the sign with passivity and at most a fleeting meaning, he turns it into a metaphor for their journey. The sign, "New Hope Church, 3 mi," is the worded hub from and beyond which they move. In investing the faded words with meaning, Darl asserts his own authority. He interprets events and is conscious of shaping our perceptions—just as a narrator is. And as long as Darl recognizes the word as "half someone else's" (Bakhtin, "Discourse in the Novel," 293), we allow his authority.

Darl's description of the fire that he sets illustrates both his inexorable ties to language and its link to his madness. Setting fire to the barn is arguably a sane act, but Darl also turns it into a linguistic event and thus strengthens the connection between narrator and madman. He tells us that Jewel runs into the fire like a "figure cut from tin" and when he struggles with Gillespie, the two "are like . . . figures in a Greek frieze, isolated out of all reality by the red glare." In the telling, Darl illustrates the way language freezes time and movement and turns the fire into a fiction. His effort is to stop the motion that he sees with metaphor. Darl says that Jewel rushes to save Addie's coffin and "the widening crimson-edged holes . . . bloom like flowers in his undershirt" (205). Altogether Darl's language turns the fire into a surreal dream, an act that both reflects the state of his mind and implicates language in his madness because Darl lives in language more completely than any of the others. Through Darl we see the negative extreme of making metaphors. Instead of simply validating the relational nature of the world, Darl's efforts begin to blur the line between reality and fiction. Paradoxically, the novel's very structure asserts that fiction *is* reality in that all the narrators exist only through their words. But their words work to connect them to an outside reality; they participate in the dialogue. Darl gradually sees everything as the product of his own articulation.

As the novel progresses, Darl's early detachment, which is common to narrators, grows into a total separation from everything, even himself. At the end, Darl is on the train going to the state asylum, and he speaks of himself in the third person: "Our brother Darl in a cage in Jackson where, his grimed hands lying in the quiet interstices, looking out he foams. 'Yes yes yes yes yes yes yes yes' " (235). Darl's words mock his position—he has become his own observer, his own author. He is going to the asylum because Dewey Dell exacts her revenge for his knowing about her pregnancy. Cash describes Darl's omniscience as being "like he could see through walls and into the next ten minutes" (219), and finally his extraperception has both abetted his madness and allowed him special comprehension of the unbearable absurdity of the entire journey to bury Addie Bundren. Whether Darl's omniscience is the result or cause of his insanity is left deliberately ambiguous, but the two are linked.[7] In effect, Darl has struggled throughout to intercept events by making them a coherent story. But ultimately his language will not allow him to control events because he is also living the story he is telling. Once he removes himself, he can be objective, but that means the dissolution of himself.

The parallels between Darl's efforts and those of a narrator or author cast fiction-making beyond ordinary endeavors. Darl's special gift lets him translate experience into language that invests it with meaning. Although Faulkner shows that interpretation is a human instinct, Darl's vision is keener and more obsessive than the other narrator's. His insanity does warn against the dangers of seeing too much and living too completely in language. Darl Bundren is the embodiment of the idea in *Mosquitoes* that a writer's "dark twin," or the book that he writes, will ultimately triumph over the writer's actual self.[8] But Darl does not stand as the ultimate indictment of authoring. Instead Faulkner involves Darl in the evolution of Cash as narrator.

The first time that Cash speaks in the novel, he explains why he has beveled the edges of Addie's coffin. He arranges his words in a list; the order reflects his carpenter's view of the world and a too-limited view of narration—arrangement of the medium yields a finished product. Before Cash's section, the other characters note his presence by the noise of his saw; he works steadily and silently outside Addie's window. From the start, Cash is solely a creature of the material world, and language is just another tool to facilitate the completion of a task. Many of the recent critical arguments about Cash have focused on refuting the earlier analyses, particularly Olga Vickery's interpretation of Cash as transforming into a wonderful person. Thus I want to separate my discussion of Cash and his transformation as much as is possible from the issue of his acquisition of any humanizing qualities other than language.[9]

While Faulkner has not made any of the Bundrens particularly well-adjusted or appealing human beings, he reveals in them crucial discussion about the power of language to forge connections among people. Cash remains limited by his own lack of sensitivity and vision, but his acquisition of verbal skill does make him less isolated from human endeavor. And the process of Cash's familiarization with language also illuminates Faulkner's inquiry into the role of a narrator.

Cash next reports an exchange he has with Jewel, who threatens to topple the coffin in his haste to load it on the wagon. Cash's words are deliberate and reasonable. In the face of Jewel's anger, he calmly repeats the beginnings of his reason for cautioning Jewel. Twice Jewel interrupts before he can finish, and the section ends with Cash's unfinished sentence, his reasoning still undelivered (86). After his work is completed, Cash stands aside from the action, his directions ignored. Although he tries to talk, his words lack authority. They also refuse to acknowledge the other's language, and the idea that all language lives in a particular, shared context.

Cash's next section follows the fiasco in the river, and again it is short and unfinished: " 'It wasn't on a balance. I told them that if they wanted it to tote and ride on a balance, they would have to' " (151). The sentence is incomplete because Cash's advice is superfluous now; ironically, the unbalanced coffin is responsible for Cash's broken leg. Between these two sections, Darl defines the nature of Cash's alienation from the word, and in doing so, persuades us that the separation is harmful. The two are speculating on Jewel's all-night adventures, and briefly the scene becomes a lesson:

> [Cash] looked at me, his eyes fumbling, the words fumbling at what he was trying to say. "It aint always the safe things in this world that a fellow . . ."
> "You mean, the safe things are not always the best things?"
> "Ay; best," he said, fumbling again. "It aint the best things; the things that are good for him. . . . A young boy. A fellow kind of hates to see . . . wallowing in somebody else's mire . . ." That's what he was trying to say. (117)

Darl then continues to explain Cash's point, a process that underscores the limitation in Cash's unfamiliarity with words and the power in Darl's greater linguistic skills. But Cash does know what he wants to say and more importantly, he wants to say it. At this point, Darl gives his thoughts words, thus establishing himself as his brother's tutor.

Darl can do this because he shares with Cash a special understanding. Darl's omniscience is a fact of the novel, but Cash's prescience is an added detail that informs our comprehension of his transformation. Darl first describes his communication with Cash as they journey toward the river: "He and I look at one another with long probing looks, looks that plunge unimpeded through one another's eyes and into the ultimate secret place" (128). Significantly, the look is an exchange; Cash shares in the insight. Darl also notes, however, that when they speak, they do not voice what they have found in each other. But the entire section hints at their special communication. Cash's powers are not as formidable as Darl's, but he can read Darl's thoughts. As they watch Jewel lift his horse into the river, Darl remembers Jewel as a baby, lying on a pillow in Addie's lap. Darl does not speak, but Cash finishes his thought: " 'That pillow was longer than him' " (130). The comment voices more than Darl's thoughts; it demonstrates a significant step in Cash's development as a narrator. Cash has access to his brother's unspoken thoughts, and this time he puts them into words.

Cash's communion with Darl grants him access to the means by which he can articulate his perceptions about the world. Cash has only two more sections in the novel, but both come after the decision has been made to send Darl to Jackson. It is Cash who explains the decision—he tells the story with authority and with a clear understanding of the relativity of sanity. Cash also exhibits a comprehension of the others that comes from his detached but newly sensitized vision. He watches Dewey Dell and knows that she told Gillespie that Darl set the barn on fire. With his sharpened perceptions of others comes a newfound assurance with language. Cash speaks without the brilliant flourishes of Darl; rather, his voice is the ordinary yet knowing voice of a man at home with his language: "I aint so sho that ere a man has the right to say what is crazy and what aint. It's like there was a fellow in every man that's done a-past the sanity or the insanity, that watches the sane and the insane doings of that man with the same horror and the same astonishment" (221). Cash's words grow increasingly literate, establishing him as a narrator we trust. His acceptance of the other, of our ability to step outside the self returns the act of narration to sanity: "That's how I reckon a man is crazy. That's how he cant see eye to eye with other folks" (216).

Appropriately, Cash's last section also ends the novel. He reports the family's movements, returning them all to the persistently mundane world in which Anse gets his new teeth and a new wife who has her own "graphophone." His words are easy and serve to move the novel toward conclusion. Cash also achieves a balance between presenting what we are to believe is an accurate view of the Bundrens and his own desire to make events meaningful. He thus can give a credible summation of Darl's fate: "But it is better so for him. This world is not his world; this life his life" (242). Ultimately, Cash's words do not signal approval of "this world," but he does accept the limitations of his family that Darl cannot.

Although Cash is not the only voice at the novel's close, he does evolve as the central advocate of the notion of language as dialogue. Cash's appropriation of language accompanies his growth into an insightful observer. Particularly significant is his comprehension that successful, i.e., meaningful, language acknowledges its own dependence upon the context of speaker and listener, or author and reader. *As I Lay Dying* argues the validity of explaining a whole through multiple perspectives, or the varied languages of fifteen narrators (Bakhtin, "Discourse in the Novel," 288–94). Mixed chronology and a constant turnover in the telling refuses an ultimate authority. Yet Faulkner does reiterate the possibilities for language to formulate, even to *be* consciousness and to connect people to the external world that they inevitably will attempt to order by their interpretations of it.

A significant thread in the novel is the dialogical mediation between Addie's rigid rejection of language and Darl's total immersion in language. Faulkner creates the dialogue in *As I Lay Dying* by giving one point of view, only to undercut it with an opposite one, and then to repeat a variation of the process. The effect is to place a higher value on language as exchange than on the word as absolute and to invite the reader to participate in Faulkner's making of the Bundren family saga into a dialogue on the process of creating narrative. Yet although Faulkner emphasizes language as the primary connector among people, he does not find an easy resolution of his anxieties about language. Soon after, he returns to confront those anxieties full force in *Light in August*.

Light in August

Near the end of Gavin Stevens' explanation of how Joe Christmas' warring blood and his grandmother's words lead him to "passively commit suicide," he describes the final rise of white blood as sending Joe "into the embrace of a chimaera, a blind faith in something read in a printed Book."[10] Gavin's nod to the dangerous powers of the word does not stop him from delivering, with authority, his own version of Joe's death. The racism in Gavin's theory of blood is unquestionable; how much of it is Faulkner's has troubled many readers of *Light in August*.[11] *Light in August* is the first novel to make race a central issue, and in doing so, it reveals more fully the disconcerting tension between Faulkner's sympathy for blacks, his clear indictment of racism, and the more subtle evidence that Faulkner himself saw black people through the filter of white culture. In one of the most coherent approaches to this tension, Myra Jehlen sees the novel as split into two conflicting parts—the complex story of Joe Christmas and the narrative vision epitomized by Gavin Stevens' theory of blood. This results from Faulkner's opposition to the unfair treatment of blacks and his own conflicting belief in their natural inferiority.[12] Most recent critics would agree at least that, for whatever reasons, Faulkner has some trouble hearing authentic black voices. But when Gavin reduces the nightmare of racism to a few paragraphs of supposition that he believes to be the truth, he also unwittingly discloses the reason we should not believe him. While Faulkner may be unable to get outside the white culture's view of black people, he explores issues of race through an indirect challenge to his own endeavor. Gavin's theory appears in a printed book; to believe it is to trust a chimaera.

The character Gail Hightower makes a similar observation in the chapter devoted to his painful but necessary soul search. When he realizes that his beautiful wife has manipulated him into marriage with her "desperate calculation," he thinks, "How false the most profound book turns out to be when applied to life" (531). As do Gavin's, Hightower's words reveal disturbing assumptions even as they undercut themselves. The observation reflects the hostility toward women that permeates *Light in August;* feminist readers will agree with Hightower, but for very different reasons of course. While I agree with those critics who argue that Faulkner shares some part of the racism and misogyny that fill this novel, I bring the issues up not to accuse or to excuse. Rather the voices of the racist and the misogynist take us straightaway to the fact that language cannot be separated from the world.[13] Hightower's words appear to challenge the very text in which they appear. They carry the same indictment of words that forms Addie Bundren's life; again they respond to the reader or writer who forgets that absolute words are dead words. Characters who undercut the enterprise that gives them life are self-conscious reminders that, as Bakhtin asserts, the word "cannot escape the profound influence of the answering words that it anticipated" ("Discourse in the Novel," 280). If we can agree with Bakhtin that the novel incorporates that fact of the spoken word into an artistic whole, then Faulkner's characters are the embodiment of the presence of response in language. And this last fact causes all sorts of trouble. Faulkner revives the issue of the dangerous inefficacy of language in *Light in August* in order to explore the most extreme implications of language as inextricable from society and history.

For a novel whose title suggests warmth and brightness, *Light in August* is about as dark as they come. However misleading the title is, it does underscore the point that illuminating an idea does not always make it completely knowable. *Light in August* is the first novel in which Faulkner places the greatest trauma in Southern and American history at the center of a text. For all the characters but Lena Grove, the external facts of historical slavery and present-day racism bear some connection to experience. As their stories are told, regional history becomes indistinguishable from personal history. The further we go into a character's past, the more complicated and larded with half-understood memories the present becomes. The novel is filled with the words of people talking about the way it is or was. We watch most of them trapped and destroyed by their versions of the world, either because what they think they know is false or because they cannot know. All of the stories are ordered, albeit unconventionally, by an omniscient narrator whose words, as critics have noted, are no less charged with social prejudices. Through the narrator, Faulkner steps back a bit from the individual consciousness to explore the ways that language functions communicably. To a much fuller extent than Darl or Cash Bundren, the narrator of *Light in August* illustrates the necessity of an awareness of the other in language and the difficulty, perhaps the impossibility, of full knowledge. A significant part of *Light in August* concerns the re-creation of memory as the key to the present; but to the exploration of private articulation, Faulkner adds public articulations in the form of prayers and codes, suggestive names, jokes, and a brilliant demonstration of his own linguistic inventiveness. The interplay between private and public language emphasizes that the process of articulating the self and experience is made truer and more difficult by the necessary acknowledgement of the other in words and lives.

Throughout *Light in August*, the narrator reiterates our connections to language, for good and bad. Everyone, even the nonverbal Lena, lives in a voiced world: "Behind her the four weeks, the evocation of *far*, is a peaceful corridor paved with unflagged and tranquil faith and peopled with kind and nameless faces and voices" (7). Several times the narrator recounts the swirl of talk surrounding Lena; and town gossip, "that single idle word blown from mind to mind" (77), fuels the downfalls of Hightower and Joe Christmas. The narrator pays attention to all the ways in which people make the world meaningful. At times it seems that everything in the world can speak. Gail Hightower listens to a church organ and hears "the apotheosis of his own history" (405). Byron Bunch chastises himself for not reading fate's warning in the yellow column of smoke from the burning Burden house. When Hightower reads Tennyson, it is to hide away from real life, but after he has officiated at Lena's delivery, he chooses to read *Henry IV*, "food for a man" (447). Shakespeare's story of the achievement of maturity is appropriate reading now; literature may have a viable place in real life after all. The novel asks what that place is and how we can know it. Hightower's faith in books as formulas for life is elsewhere proven false, and he, Joe Christmas, and Joanna Burden latch onto codes (absolute words) that overwhelm their lives. In each case, the words only become absolute codes when the listener's response transforms them.

Hightower has trapped himself inside an old story of his grandfather's dubious heroics in the Civil War. In a terrible irony, of which Faulkner may not have been aware, the young Gail hears of his Yankee-killing grandfather from the black woman who ran his father's home. The bridge between her voice and the old uniform becomes his pride and his prison. To double his imprisonment, he preaches "dogma . . . all full of galloping calvary and defeat and glory" (67). Religion becomes a worded haven for him, "like a classic and serene vase" (528), which of course his involvement with Lena and Byron ultimately shatters. The Keatsian allusion recalls the prison Horace Benbow creates in *Flags* in his desire to live undisturbed in language. Hightower also tries to hide in books, first reading Tennyson's "fine galloping language [because] it is better than praying without having to bother to think aloud. It is like listening in a cathedral to a eunuch chanting in a language which he does not even need to not understand" (350). Here Hightower demonstrates the same self-mocking attitude that makes Horace, Quentin, and Faulkner's other intellectuals doubly ineffectual. Awareness of the sterility of his belief in words makes Hightower's defeat more painful, but it is also predictable; he can talk about his problem but cannot change it.

An even stronger indictment against unquestioning and total commitment to the word comes in the characterization of Joe Christmas and Joanna Burden. The word *Negro* burdens Joanna and dooms Joe before he can even understand its meaning: "Memory believes before knowing remembers. Believes longer than recollects, longer than knowing even wonders" (131). Through the articulation of Joe's childhood memories, the narrator recreates the pasts that both Joe and Joanna carry with them. Both have invested their lives in the words of their fathers.

Two men stand in place of the father Joe never knows. Both men claim the Bible as the Word by which they live, and both are rigid and mean-spirited as a result. Doc Hines calls his grandson "a sign and a damnation for bitchery" (140); Joe is for him nothing but an idea. His belief in signs is a perversion of the human need to find meaning in the world. Hines' need to punish his daughter causes him to turn to the Word of God, becoming God's vengeful crusader against "womansinning and bitchery" (141). Joe may have heard Hines' venomous names for females just as he apparently first hears from him the word *nigger*. In any case, Joe's misogyny is guaranteed by the time he faces the distraught dietitian. Echoing Hines' habit of doubling into one word the name of his hatred, "womanfilth" (145), the narrator joins Joe's fear of women to his fear of being black. He stands in Freedman Town and "on all sides, even within him, the bodiless fecundmellow voices of negro women murmured. It was as though he and all other manshaped life about him had been returned to the lightless hot wet primogenitive female" (126). The language of this and countless other passages in *Light in August* is charged with such sexual and racial terror that it in effect becomes the nightmarish threat of the other.[14]

The words of Joe's other father, McEachern, also form his responses. McEachern is a more stringent biblical scholar than Hines. The episode in which he tries literally to beat the Presbyterian catechism into Joe also comments grimly on the transformation of the Word into an inflexible code, the dicta of a vengeful God. After he beats Joe, McEachern prays over him, "his voice droning, soporific, monotonous" (167). His prayers are lifeless and remain unanswered. Later McEachern delivers his pronouncement about all things tainted by sin, from town restaurants to all of womankind. His words do not necessarily teach Joe to trust language, although he does see women as vessels of his own sin, but they do teach Joe that language is a precept and carries an unbending authority. Joe internalizes the voices of his two fathers (the ultimate voice of authority) to feed his fears, just as Quentin

Compson does. Also like Quentin, Joe is acutely aware of voices everywhere, and of himself as composed of voices: "voices evocative of names and times and places . . . which were his life" (115). Joe too warns of the potential prison in the printed word—giving Saussurean privilege to the spoken word: "thinking *God perhaps and me not knowing that too* He could see it like a printed sentence, fullborn and already dead" (115). But for Joe, all words are a threat because he has no word to call himself except the one he hates. He is alienated from others' words because he sees them only as absolute impositions. Thus his explanation for killing Joanna: "It's because she started praying over me."

Joanna's strange and terrible life tells us again of the dangerous authority in another's words. Aptly named, as are all the characters, Joanna Burden is burdened by a family legacy of responsibility as only a New England Calvinist can understand the word. Joanna's grandfather was named Calvin Burden and when her father takes her to see his grave, he voices a family doom, which is also "the curse of every white child that ever was born and that ever will be born" (239). His words lock Joanna into a tortured penance and a reverence for the word that eventually kills her.

But Joanna is also a woman, and that fact facilitates her demise as much as does her assumption of the family curse. Sexual and racial hostility are joined most grotesquely when in the nyphomaniacal frenzy that Joe's rape of her triggers, Joanna cries "Negro! Negro! Negro!" (285). Here it seems clear that the narrator shares Joe's misogyny, and Faulkner's reliance on sexual stereotypes can be seen as evidence of his own participation in cultural attitudes about female sexuality as fearsome.[15] Robert Parker reads the novel's excessive language as parodic, an important move beyond Faulkner's complicity in his characters' prejudices, to focus on the connections between them and language. Parker argues that to see Joe and Joanna as parodies of male and female stereotypes is to give Faulkner more control over the language that often seems out of control; he rightfully notes Faulkner's sensitivity to language, especially the rhetoric of types. Beyond the issue of where the sexist and racist language originates is the fact that it illustrates the tension between the self and the other in language. At any point in the lurid description of Joanna's passage from ice maiden to aging vixen to menopausal wreck, the language presents a woman fixed in the nightmare of female extremes. Joanna is trapped by what she, Joe, and the narrator think female is. Ultimately, they all speak with one voice. However unaware he is of his own participation in the voice, Faulkner is aware of the dangers of shutting dialogue out of language. In the story of Joe and Joanna, Faulkner puts the flaming rhetoric of Doc Hines into action. Both characters are trapped inside definitions of *woman* and *Negro* that are absolute and bear the most negative and extreme psychosocial burdens. Joe and Joanna, as well as Hightower, live out society's most limiting definitions of their lives.

The implacable presence of Lena Grove is often taken as Faulkner's alternative to those characters who accept absolutely another's words. Hightower apparently voices the core of Lena's existence in his question, " 'What are a few mumbled words before God, before the steadfastness of a woman's nature?' " (337). Critics of Lena argue, I think correctly, that she embodies the patriarchal notion of woman-as-womb.[16] But Lena's affinity with the wordless and dependable cycles of nature is not an absolute answer to the overworded existences of the others.

A closer look at Lena reveals her own paradoxical tie to the word. Tired of waiting for Lucas Burch's "mouthword," she starts off to find the father of her baby. She says they need "no word promises" (22), but she obviously is determined to make his word good. She tells Will Varner the story of her impending marriage "with the patient and transparent recapitulation of a lying child" (27). While Lena's nature is more attuned than the others to the romantic female life principle, she determines to hold Burch to his word and to lie her way to him. The lie, however, is that Burch is her husband, not that she believes he will be. Lena knows when to be ready with an explanation, although her words always appear disconnected from life. The deputy who finds Lena in the cabin on the Burden property reports that " 'she began telling me almost before I got inside the cabin, like it was a speech. Like she had done got used to telling it, done got into the habit' " (351). Saying the words by rote, Lena demonstrates pragmatism rather than a disregard for language. Faulkner's readers know that he consistently attributes that pragmatism to the female because of his belief in her greater involvement with the physical rather than the intellectual world. Joanna Burden, the abolitionist who tries too late to have a child is described as looking increasingly "mannish." On the other hand, Lena's unspoiled, natural insight and a few well-chosen words help her to strip Lucas Burch of "verbiage and deceit" (477) when they finally meet. Quickly Lena realizes that Lucas lies about what he has done and cannot articulate his real fears. Her straightforward questions about his intentions cut through his excuses; Lena holds him "with something against which his lying blew trivial as leaves of trash" (477). Their exchange underscores the inefficacy of empty words in the face of honest and direct ones. But Lena's placid surrender of her belief in Burch's "promise" is so uncomplicated that it moves her more completely into the realm of male myth.[17]

Throughout the novel, associations of Lena with the fecund, unintelligent earth makes her less a human than an idea. She is "like something moving forever and without progress across an urn" (7), another allusion to Keats that links Lena with the things men create as art. To Byron Bunch and even to Hightower, Lena is an ideal and idea more than she is a woman. More significantly, her characterization is so uncomplicated and exaggerated that she is clearly an idea for the narrator as well. Thus her story ends the novel enclosed inside the furniture dealer's story. The chapter calls attention to itself as story, opening like the traditional fairy tale, "There lives in the eastern part of the state a furniture repairer and dealer" (545), and ending in classic comic resolution. Of all of the characters, Lena is most self-consciously the narrator's creation. As a creature of the imagination, Lena asserts an idea contradictory to the role she plays within the novel. She embodies the narrator's and even Byron's impulse to turn her into the articulation of an idea, and she is the positive but equally closed definition of woman. Under no circumstances would I argue that Faulkner was a feminist, but he was at least partially aware that Lena Grove was the projection of a masculine consciousness. As such, she is most strongly connected to the other characters, for she also embodies the warning that our potential for isolation is strongest in our desire for the absolute word.

The stories of Gail Hightower, Joe Christmas, and Joanna Burden all carry an indictment of a belief in language that refuses to acknowledge its conditional, experiential nature. Lena appears to be an acceptable alternative to the absolute power the others invest in language, but as the narrator's worded ideal, she too is monologic. The impulse to trust language absolutely isolates everyone. With names like Joe Christmas and Joanna Burden, Faulkner acknowledges but only partially mocks his own belief in the power of words. In no other novel does he invest so much potential meaning in the names he gives his characters. We are asked to note that Lena Grove's name conjures a deceptively correct association with natural things and that Reverend Hightower apt ly describes his deliberate efforts to remove himself from life. Thei. after he witnesses the birth of Lena's baby, we see that Hightower wishes to be its namesake, as if the naming will solidify his connection to life. Joe's first disastrous involvement with a woman is cast in the echoes of the old ballad of "bonny Barbara Allen." The allusion does enrich the episode because the difference between Bobbie Allen and her namesake comment ironically on romantic love.[18] Conversely yet characteristically, Lucas Burch slips in and out of names like clothes. Also known as Lucas Brown and Joe Brown, Burch tries to keep his identity fluid, and, just as all his lies do, changing his name only marks him as manipulative and untrustworthy. Joe's name, coupled with details like his being left on the orphanage steps on Christmas Day and being martyred at thirty-three invite the obvious analogy to Jesus Christ, but the analogy is tenuous, even if it is ironic, as many readers argue. Yet what seems to be just a self-conscious literary device actually calls our attention to the novel's central subject. Upon first hearing Joe's name, Byron Bunch articulates the belief system we bring to the naming process:

A man's name, which is supposed to be just the sound for who he is, can be somehow an augur for what he will do, if other men can only read the meaning in time. It seemed to him that none of them had looked especially at the stranger until they heard his name. . . .

it was as though there was something in the sound of it that was trying to tell them what to expect. (35)

Light in August is about the difficulties of reading people correctly, of knowing when people lie and when they tell the truth, of negotiating in a world of mixed and deceptive communications. The idea that a name is destiny or somehow the key to understanding its bearer is powerful enough that the narrator cannot expose it as complete sham. The Christmas-Christ analogy is present, perhaps as a red herring and perhaps as one key to interpreting Joe's unredeemed life. Faulkner's characters are texts themselves, but more often than not they are closed off from each other (the Grove, Bunch, and Hightower stories are only tangentially connected to Joe and Joanna). The narrator makes repeated references to the many voices in this world, but nearly always the voices lie or fall on deaf ears. In spite of the acknowledged other in language, communication seems nearly impossible.

Byron Bunch also wrestles with the problem of negotiating the tensions between the self and the multivoiced world. He comes closer to resolution than any other character, and in doing so, he points the way to the novel's approach to the limitations of language. Byron realizes when Lena's baby is born that he has convinced himself of her sexual innocence. He achieves his remarkable belief simply by declaring the lie in all evidence to the contrary: *"[We] were just a lot of words that never even stood for anything, not even us, while all the time what was us was going on and going on without even missing the lack of words"* (443–44). By making everything up to the birth "just a lot of words," Byron tries vainly to deny the reality of Lucas Burch. Accompanying Byron's recognition of Burch is an understanding of the impossibility of achieving absolutes through language. He comes to this awareness by listening to the "inescapable horizons of the implacable earth" (468). The hills are the only absolutes, and they do speak to Byron:

> You say you suffer. All right. But in the first place, all we got is your naked word for it. And in the second place, you just say that you are Byron Bunch. And in the third place, you are just the one that calls yourself Byron Bunch today, now, this minute. (468)

Byron's involvement with Lena ultimately proves to him the lie in trying to substitute word for deed or for a tested belief. And in his communication with the hills, Byron spells out the insignificance and transience of his own word. But Byron is responsible for the entire communication; he accepts the presence of the other. From this acceptance comes his resolution to try to follow through with his involvement with Lena. His effort is to make his word good in the face of daunting limitations.

The novel as a whole mirrors Byron's struggle to make good the word. Belief or disbelief in the efficacy of language informs the struggles of all the major characters. In addition, the narrator perpetuates the dialectic by uncovering the emptiness of words and then turning around to underscore their power. On the one hand, he tells of how easily words can lie, isolate, and imprison. On the other, he continually reiterates the positive power of telling, whether through the recreation of the past or the final enclosure of Lena and Byron into story. *Light in August* also presents one of Faulkner's most masterful demonstrations of his power as a stylist. Words like "Augusttremulous" and "day-granaried" do more than evoke beautifully precise, yet abstract notions about a day and a leaf. They tell of Faulkner's love for what language would allow him to describe, order, and create. *Light in August* brilliantly illustrates Bakhtin's argument that traditional stylistics, with its orientation toward unity, is inadequate to discuss the heteroglossia of novelistic language. The novel, Bakhtin says, does not talk straight; the life in language comes out of its employment of "forms that orchestrate their themes by means of languages" ("Discourse in the Novel," 275). In the language Faulkner creates are compound words like *brassridged, violenthaired*, (194, 195) and others that fill the novel. In the act of making new words from "old" ones, Faulkner borrows a technique from James Joyce and takes personal control over his medium. Olga Vickery refers to this as making a "communal" language private.[19] But Faulkner's compounds do more than assert his power as author; they also open language to the possibilities for new, more precise meanings. The effect of words like "sootbleakened," "sparrowlike childtrebling," and "grassless cinder-strewnpacked compound" (131) is to strike us with the amplitude of ordinary experience and with the language that brings us its fullness. We also recognize anew that the malleability of language is also positive; it can give us the power to see the world more clearly.

Often Faulkner will stretch words into new parts of speech, making a verb into a noun or an adjective into a verb to create a sense of action, as in the "yearly adjacenting chimneys" of Joe Christmas' orphanage (131). Faulkner's license with conventional usage frees words from their established and thus potentially numbing definitions. He tells us that words are not permanently fixed objects, that they are creations of the human mind and they are alive in the world. The opening of chapter 6, "Memory believes before knowing remembers," gives us a language that doesn't talk straight. We have to stop to be sure that we understand what the words are saying. And when we do and then read the story of Joe's past, we witness how precisely Faulkner has orchestrated his themes by means of languages.

While the characters' stories unfold to disclose the dangers and falseness of language, the sum of the novel's many voices celebrates the power of its languages and allows Faulkner to restructure our assumptions about reading and thus about language. If we believe, as Hightower does, that books contain absolutes or even formulas for living, we will be surprised continually by "how false the most profound book turns out to be when applied to life" (531). Faulkner suggests something far more radical, especially in light of his repeated warnings about language. A novel is not a guide for life, nor is it just a mirror of life. Rather, a novel *is* life, or at least an important part of life. A novel engages our thought and activates our memory by articulating the thoughts and memories of other people, including the author. *Light in August* is about the process of living in the multivoiced world, of trying to understand and respond to its languages. The novel makes us aware of our own vulnerabilities as readers by giving us characters whose potential for misreading seems infinite. Yet the re-creation of Joe Christmas' past and Gail Hightower's memories do attempt to explain both men. The narrator refuses conclusive definitions of any of the characters, however. Hightower's fate, Joe's racial heritage, and the future of Byron and Lena remain ambiguous. Even Joanna Burden, whose fate is clear, escapes absolute definition precisely because she is created in language that makes her deceptively stereotypical.

A brief look at one other, deceptively simple technique illuminates Faulkner's method of keeping language alive by demonstrating its multiplicity—the joke. The joke in *Light in August* is significant first of all because the same idea is reworded to fit four different circumstances in the novel. The crux of the joke rests on the subject's inability to know a situation beforehand, or to read "correctly." At its first telling, the joke lends a comic tone to Lena's pregnant predicament—she's not just unwed, but deserted as well. What normally is a very difficult situation is for Lena simply the way life is. Now with child, Lena remarks on her struggle to climb through the window that had earlier provided her escape to Lucas: " 'If it had been this hard to do before, I reckon I would not be doing it now' " (6). The next time the joke appears it takes on a much darker tone. When Byron recounts to Hightower Lucas Burch's story of moving Joanna Burden's body, he includes the following ghoulish detail: "The cover fell open and she was lying on her side, facing one way, and her head was turned clean around like she was looking behind her. And he said how if she could just have done that when she was alive, she might not have been doing it now" (101). The words evoke a mixture of horror and amusement similar to the effect of Jason Compson's jokes about his family. Laughter is possible because we do not at this point know Joanna, but the joke also uncovers a bit of truth. If Joanna had understood herself and Joe Christmas perhaps she could have saved herself.

The same rueful awareness of possible misreading lies behind Joe Christmas' comment to Joanna: " 'If I'm not [black], damned if I haven't wasted a lot of time' " (280). Joe's joke reveals a momentary insight that his convictions otherwise erase, but his words reiterate the potential for alternative readings that threaten complete resolution. The joke appears a final time in the furniture dealer's narration of Lena and Byron. This narrator asserts his own power as teller by claiming superior knowledge of Byron's situation with Lena. All the details of Byron's frustration and timidity build to his venture into the truck to accost the sleeping Lena. The dealer observes, " 'Old boy, if you'd a just done this last night, you'd a been sixty miles further south than you are now . . . And if you'd a done it two nights ago, I reckon I wouldn't ever have laid eyes on either one of you' " (554). But both the dealer and Byron have misread the situation, and Lena is not to be conquered by masculine assertiveness. The language takes some of the edge off the fact that the dealer and his wife are chuckling over an attempted rape.

In all four situations the joke undercuts, however briefly, the solemnity of a serious scene, as if to catch us before we invest the situation with too exclusive an interpretation. The jokes embody perfectly the doubleness of language that *Light in August* desires to exploit. The joke is about the hazards of not knowing and the potential for misreading, yet inherent in its telling is a belief in the power of language to facilitate comprehension. *Light in August* makes the process of articulation a complicated and necessary human concern precisely because it explores its varied dangers. The novel is as concerned as *The Sound and the Fury* and *As I Lay Dying* with the individual's connection to language, but it extends that concern into the realm of communication, or the confrontation with the other's words. *Light in August* tells us that living in the world is like reading or even writing a book. People engage themselves in language out of need and desire, and their living is a process of negotiating among memories, conscious and preconscious thought, present conditions and the words of others. *Light in August* does warn of certain dangers, but it offers no guide except the implicit belief that living is the search for meaning, the process of articulation, the effort to read—and not the resolution.

4
Ike McCaslin
and the
Threatened Order

In the boy's eyes at least it was Sam Father's, the negro,
who bore himself not only toward his cousin McCaslin and
Major de Spain but toward all white men, with gravity and
dignity and without servility or recourse to that impen-
etrable wall of ready and easy mirth which negroes sustain
between themselves and white men.

That chronicle . . . was a whole land in miniature, which
multiplied and compounded, was the entire South.—*Go
Down, Moses*

In the ten years between the publication of *Light in August*
and *Go Down, Moses* (1942), Faulkner had returned to America's
legacy of slavery in both *Absalom, Absalom!* and *The Unvanquished* (1938), but *Go Down, Moses* marks a change in the telling.
Much in its composition and theme appears familiar: separate
stories and rearranged chronology emphasize the fragmented and
multivoiced world in which characters negotiate between past and
present, and the curse of racial division haunts the present and
threatens the future. *Go Down, Moses* also includes two white
characters who try to articulate and thereby control, and even
erase, the tortured legacy of racial guilt and fear. It is in Isaac
McCaslin, and to a lesser extent in Gavin Stevens, that Faulkner's
own anxieties about race and writing converge.

Both of these characters, as well as Horace, Quentin, and Darl, seek the safety of absolutes and, correspondingly, want words to be what they name. The strength of that desire again removes the characters too far from the multivoiced world. With Ike McCaslin, Faulkner incorporates the same desires into a larger, more elemental struggle with nature and God, set inside the trauma of racial fears and hatreds. The movement of Ike's life and Faulkner's account of it in *Go Down, Moses* is toward a sublime, wordless communion with *the absolute* that can be approached only through language. As a result, Ike's involvement with language is weightier, although not more intense than Quentin's. The tension between Ike's belief and disbelief manifests itself as more fundamental and more universal. Ike's conflict shapes itself around his belief in and reliance upon language and his desire to reach a communication with nature and God that is beyond all words. All five characters yearn, in part, to get beyond language, but only Ike seeks transcendence rather than escape.

Yet that very desire betrays Ike's irrevocable ties to a land and people who defy his every effort to move above the chaos they have created. Faulkner links the exploitation of the land to the white man's exploitation of blacks and through Ike in particular appears to condemn white paternalism.[1] But the assumption of white entitlement is harder to escape than perhaps even Faulkner imagined or understood. The absolute language, the truth of the human heart, to which Ike aspires is a language of authority. The words themselves help to reify our culture's patriarchal values. Old Ben, symbol of the natural world, is several times compared to a locomotive; the McCaslin legacy, symbol of the patrilineal culture, is an old coffee pot stuffed with IOUs. Ike also believes in universals, for example that the land is "bigger and older than any recorded document"[2] and thus is separate from the values that threaten it. The romantic idea of the pristine natural world extant for human needs belies its own genesis in the very culture it seeks to transcend. The narrative effort of *Go Down, Moses* is to detach from the culture and thus the horrors of slavery and capitalism while implicitly presenting them as excesses of an essentially good and true order. The effort mirrors Ike's faith in the absolute truths of God and nature, faith both ennobles and threatens Ike's struggle. The absolute truths of *Go Down, Moses* are, as Myra Jehlen has shown, not so much universal as they are white.[3] Citing Zack Edmonds' rescue of Lucas Beauchamp's elaborate plot to get rid of George Wilkins, Jehlen exposes the aspects of Lucas' characterization that connect him to cultural stereotypes of the "lovable darky." She makes the central point about Lucas, who is Faulkner's most complex and dignified black, when she notes the connection between his power and the ideals of manhood that are universalized in the novel. Even Lucas himself identifies his positive attributes—self-reliance, fiscal responsibility, and courage—with his "white blood." Gavin Stevens' theory of blood echoes in Lucas' extended references in the section "The Fire and the Hearth" to his standing up to Edmonds as the acting out of "old Carothers' blood" (58). Yet it is Lucas, not Ike, who accomplishes the act of self-creation, itself a patriarchal value, that the entire novel aspires to. "Self-progenitive and nominate," (281) Lucas renames and thus creates himself—the power of the word appears absolute here. The novel both tries to establish that same power and challenges it repeatedly.

The dialogue between Ike and Cass Edmonds in the commissary is a model for the dialogue about language embedded in the whole of *Go Down, Moses*. Cass adds to and periodically attempts to revise Ike's monologue. We know that Cass' words are true; his role as responder underlines Faulkner's belief in the word's "double-voicedness" (Bakhtin, "Discourse in the Novel," 328). But Ike's narrative and his desire for the power of transforming his words into *the word* overshadows Cass' contribution—even though Cass' prediction that Ike can never be free of his heritage is proven true. The stakes involved in Ike's repudiation are too high and too laden with guilt and fear to be easily assimilated into any compromise. Ike and Cass achieve no "happy marriage of speaking and hearing" (*Absalom*, 316). Ike strains toward single-voicedness. And even as he recognizes the multivoiced world, in *Go Down, Moses*, Faulkner feels the strain as well. Ike's struggle is similar to Faulkner's; the power in language seduces both.

In "The Old People" section, we learn that Ike is very young when he first listens to Sam Fathers' stories about the past. Sam teaches Ike much more than how to hunt, because to know the wilderness he must know its past. Sam's stories affect Ike in much the same way that the stories of Thomas Sutpen affect Quentin Compson. In both cases, the boys incorporate what they hear into their own lives. Ike learns early the power of language:

> Gradually to the boy those old times would cease to be old times and would become part of the boy's present, not only as if they had happened yesterday but as if they were still happening . . . as if some of them not happened yet but would occur tomorrow, until at last it would seem to the boy that he himself had not come into existence yet . . . and that it was he, the boy, who was the guest here and Sam Father's [sic] voice the mouthpiece of the host. (71)

Sam's stories blur the line between present and past until Ike's temporal existence is wiped away. The stories also blur the line between experience and story for Ike: "The boy even at almost eighty would never be able to distinguish certainly between what he had seen and what had been told him" (291). We are to understand that Ike is not just enthralled by a master storyteller; he is in the presence of the "mouthpiece of the host," which in biblical terms makes of Sam a symbol similar to the consecrated bread of the Eucharist. Sam speaks for the original dwellers of the wilderness, and Ike invests his words with enough power to disallow his own family's claim on the land. Sam's words take Ike out of the confines of his own present and make him a part of a timeless, paradoxical "truth," that the wilderness cannot be owned yet exists for men's use, particularly as a measure of manhood. When Ike is ten, he finds that Sam's words have already acclimated him to the rituals of the hunt: "It was not even strange to him. He had experienced it all before, and not merely in dreams" (195–96). While Quentin is pulled, with a mixture of fascination and dread, into Thomas Sutpen's story, Ike McCaslin willingly adopts Sam Fathers' history as his own. Even when Cass later interrupts to correct Ike's narrative, for instance when he reminds him of Sam's own obsession with racial purity, Ike is resistant to much alteration. The young boy who could be transported so completely into the past grows into the man who puts his faith in language as the means to get at the truth that he knows rests in the past. Language becomes the key that will lead Ike into the past and to the original, absolute truth.

When Sam Fathers actually speaks in "The Old People" and "The Bear," his sentences are simple and direct. Although Sam is not given to explanation, Ike invests his few words with great significance. As Ike grows older, the communication with Sam grows sparser and stronger. At the end of "The Bear," Ike thinks of Sam, buried now two years: *"He probably knew I was in the woods this morning long before I got here"* (328). Ike believes in communication beyond words, and even beyond death. He associates this purity of communication with an absolute, a source of all truth that is God. Language to Ike is the medium that links God to humans; therefore, it partakes of the divine and is flawed by the mortal. When Ike explains to his cousin McCaslin why the land cannot be bought or owned, he also reveals his belief in the Bible as the Word of God: " 'Bought nothing. Because He told in the Book how He created the earth' " (*Go Down, Moses*, 257). Although Ike believes that the Bible is the source, he gets caught on the issue of the fallibility of those who transcribed God's Word. The following, often-quoted passage is important here because it reveals how Ike maneuvers between his belief in the Bible as truth and his knowledge of the Bible as lie:

> "There are some things He said in the Book, and some things reported of Him that He did not say. And I know what you will say now: That if truth is one thing to me and another thing to you, how will we choose which is truth? The heart already knows." (260)

Ike's explanation is finally specious, but it comes out of his faith in absolutes. He believes that the heart, which he views as a collective noun, possesses the ability to discern the truth from lies. But he then explains that the same human heart caused the transcribers to alter God's Word when they put it into human language:

> "What they were trying to tell, what He said, was too simple. Those for whom they transcribed His words could not have believed Him. It had to be expounded in the everyday terms which they were

familiar with and could comprehend, not only those who listened but those who told it too, because if they who were that near to Him as to have been elected from all who breathed and spoke language to transcribe and relay His words, could comprehend truth only through the complexity of passion and lust and hate and fear which drives the heart, what distance back to truth must they traverse whom truth could only reach by word-of-mouth?" (*Go Down, Moses*, 260)

Ike's theory suggests that our complex life and language obscures the simplicity of God's truth. Like Horace, Ike explains that lying is not deceitful but rather a human compulsion. And because "passion and lust and hate and fear" are real, lying is also a form of truth.

But human realities are more complicated than God's truth. *Go Down, Moses* also contains a reference to Gavin Stevens' project to translate the Bible into classical Greek; both he and Ike seek the original Word of God, and both believe in its simplicity. But they reach for it differently. Gavin reaches through supposedly purer forms of language, Ike through a wordless intuition. Gavin's presence in the title story is generally read as Faulkner's attempt to illustrate the remaining gulf between whites and blacks. Mollie Beauchamp renders Gavin a pale facilitator of her anguished mission both through her will to get her grandson's body home and buried and in her rearrangement of the Bible story that explains Samuel's death for her: " 'Roth Edmonds sold my Benjamin. Sold him in Egypt. Pharaoh got him—' " (371). Eric Sundquist's reading of *Go Down, Moses* as the product of Faulkner's tortured racial conscience and actual social change is one of the most provocative and convincing I have read.[4] He makes the point that Gavin's part, as well as the final story's shift away from the Edmonds and McCaslin families as the locus of white grief and guilt, reflects Faulkner's failure to imagine resolution to the problems he explores. But Sundquist's puzzlement over Faulkner's continuing fascination with Gavin can be resolved by placing Gavin in the context of Faulkner's sense of uncertainty about language and about white-black relations. The separation Faulkner anguishes over between black and white Americans is, in effect, a metaphor for his acknowledged desire to maintain discreteness between his words and the world that threatens to alter them. Gavin is a kind of black-and-white thinker; the ridiculousness of his twenty-two-year-old unfinished translation of the Old Testament, particularly in the face of Aunt Mollie's real-life alteration of one of its stories does tell us that Faulkner recognized the dangers of such thinking. But Faulkner also knows that he shares more with Gavin than with Mollie, and that his desire to establish the absolute word also endangers his ability to understand the black voice.

Gavin is, however, a relatively minor character, and to strengthen my argument I turn again to Ike McCaslin. Ike also sees words as vehicles to the truth, and the connection between this idea and the Bible is more fully developed in his characterization. According to Ike, words represent truths larger than they, which the human heart mysteriously recognizes and separates from the lies. Cass tempers Ike's absolutism with a necessary skepticism when he answers Ike's question about how much time the translation of truth into language would take: " 'No time at all if, as you say, the heart knows the truth, the infallible and unerring heart' " (Go Down, Moses, 261). Ike says that the same heart that knows the truth is also responsible for the lies, but he does not explain how it perceives the difference. Although contradiction mars Ike's theory of biblical authenticity, it serves to illustrate how Ike's own search for simple truth leads him into further complexity. And major contributors to the complexity are Ike's dual belief that language tells the truth and that it tells lies. According to Ike, words are the vehicle to the truth, yet they also become the truth itself. The heart creates the lies but knows the truth. Ike declares the heart's ability to make absolute distinctions with the conviction that his saying so makes it true. For every objection Cass makes, Ike has an explanation. His words are impervious to doubt, at least to him. We, however, are meant to remember the heart's subjectivity and the word's double-voicedness. Significantly, all discussion of truth and translation centers on the writer. Interpretation by a reader is never a real part of the issue.

While Ike works to establish his version of the McCaslin story as truth, he anticipates Cass' objections. Again, dialogue keeps us aware of the presence of the other in language. For Ike, the voice is not altogether welcome. The dialogue between Ike and Cass soon becomes an illustration of the historian's task. Whatever his methodology, the historian ultimately puts some part of the past into words. Like a historian, Ike sifts through documents (the ledger), artifact (the coffee pot filled with IOUs), and his own memory to put the truth of his past (which is also the South's past) into words. Implicit in the endeavor is the belief that the words reveal the truth. The longer Ike continues, the clearer it becomes to us that the truth is not simple at all. Reflecting that fact, the language of section 4 of "The Bear" is some of the densest Faulkner ever wrote. In *A World Elsewhere*, Richard Poirier offers an important, if brief discussion of how the language of "The Bear" induces the reader to feel Ike's entrance into history via the woods.[5] Complementing Poirier's point that Faulkner's style works to suspend time for the reader is the fact that Ike also works to make the past live through his own narrative. "Maybe" prefaces most of Ike's explanations about the passage of the land from God to Ikkemotubbe to old Carothers McCaslin, yet the cumulative effect of Ike's sentences is to present a convincing history. Ike and Cass engage in the same kind of speculative effort that Quentin and Shreve do, and their words create a similar verisimilitude. To piece the story together authoritatively, Ike turns to his grandfather's ledgers, which are introduced in language that encourages their association with the Bible:

> To [Ike] it was as though the ledgers in their scarred cracked leather bindings were being lifted down one by one in their fading sequence and spread open on the desk or perhaps upon some apocryphal Bench or even Altar or perhaps before the Throne Itself for the last perusal and contemplation and refreshment of the Allknowledgeable before the yellow pages and the brown thin ink in which was recorded the injustice and a little at least of its amelioration and restitution faded back forever into the anonymous communal original dust. (*Go Down, Moses*, 261)

Clearly, Ike believes that the ledgers contain the truth, even that they are a secular version of the Word that will explain the ways of humans to God. The passage also emphasizes that the ledgers are just on the verge of disintegration. The phrase "fading sequence" underscores the idea that the books order experience and that the order is wearing away. The word is subject to temporal damage, but that seems to matter little here. The "Allknowledgeable" suggests God, but Ike is the one who takes the ledgers down to peruse. We also learn that when he does, "he knew what he was going to find before he found it" (268). And in confirmation of that, we read the ledger entries before we read of Ike's midnight visit to the ledgers. Ike goes to them for confirmation of knowledge he apparently has already divined. The "anonymous, communal original dust" suggests that written history, because it is temporal, is only a transitory construction. That fact makes the effort more urgent and more necessary. The language here suggests a God-like quality in Ike's endeavor, and at the very least, it reiterates the significance of returning to the record of the past.

The act of reading the ledgers both verifies Ike's premonitions about his grandfather and breathes life into the names from his past. The entries by Buck and Buddy McCaslin about "Percavil Brownly" evolve into a spirited dialogue that tells Ike as much about the twins as it does about Percival.[6] In perhaps the longest (three-page) separation between a subject and a verb in an English sentence, the narrator finally tells us that the twins "took substance and even a sort of shadowy life with their passions and complexities too as page followed page and year year" (266). The entries, which are simple, shorthand versions of events, disclose a great deal of life themselves, but the narrator cannot let them speak alone. Throughout, we read the embellishments of Ike's thoughts as he adds details and explanations to the entries. The three pages develop out of the belief that history and writing are collaborative processes. They also weight the ledgers with significance, and thus reinforce Ike's view of them as the source of the truth.

The ledgers were always on the edges of Ike's consciousness when he was young. We are told that as a boy he thought he might read them only when he was old and "perhaps even bored a little since what the old books contained would be after all these years fixed immutably, finished, unalterable, harmless" (268). The succession of words that underscore the idea that language nails down reality builds to a fine irony in the word *harmless*. Again we see the desire of Gavin, Quentin, and Horace inverted and exposed. Language is supposed to separate emotions, ideas, and even events out of temporal existence and fix them forever. But in the yellowing paper and fading ink, Ike sees a concrete sign that the words, and what they mean, are not immutable. The words in the old ledgers are also neither "finished" nor "harmless," for they shape the life of Ike McCaslin as profoundly as the words of Sam Fathers do. Whether or not Ike actually knows what the ledgers contain, he needs to read them. The words confirm and give substance to whatever he has intuited about his past. Ike's renunciation of his inheritance is an attempt to prove the lie in his grandfather's assumptions about ownership of the land and people. But the words ultimately double back on themselves. In "Delta Autumn," we see seventy-year-old Uncle Ike stand face to face with the legacy of miscegenation and slavery that he repudiates in "The Bear." The word is made flesh in Jim Beauchamp's granddaughter and the child she had by Roth Edmonds. Together, they force Ike to confront the fact that his renunciation has changed nothing.

Critics have thoroughly discussed the implications of Ike's discovery in "Delta Autumn," and my interest is not in whether Ike is right or wrong to live as he does. For my purposes, the significance of Ike's meeting with the young mulatto lies in the fact that it proves the boy Ike correct. The words in the ledger really are "unalterable." For Ike, the faded entries contain a shameful family legacy that epitomizes a larger human tragedy: "that chronicle . . . was a whole land in miniature" (293), exactly what *Go Down, Moses* aspires to be. Ike sets out to atone for the entries, and the fact that he does not succeed suggests the paradoxical horror of language. The words are not "finished" or "harmless," but they are "unalterable." The words lie and they tell the truth. And Ike McCaslin's heart does not know the difference.

Ike's confrontation with the power and instability of language suggests, as J. Douglas Canfield argues, that Ike McCaslin's story tells of his failed attempt to make words transcend human confusion. Canfield further states that Faulkner's voice merges with Ike's and the author's complicity indicates his own need to believe that words can, after all, conjure the lost truths humans seek so desperately.[7] Canfield fails to note that Faulkner is aware of this need, for while he shows language as a mythologizing agent, he also mythologizes the paradox of language through Ike McCaslin. The conflict between believing in the power of words and believing they are poor, untrustworthy substitutes emerges as more significant than resolving the conflict. At one point in the long dialogue in "The Bear," Ike lists among the ineffectual people who could not have instigated the Civil War the "loud rabble of the camp-followers of pioneers: the bellowing of politicians, the mellifluous choiring of self-styled men of God" (287). He speaks with derision of the empty and ineffective words of the two inherently forensic groups and, although he denies it, his words also justify the white Southerners who went to battle against "a power with ten times the area and a hundred times the men and a thousand times the resources" (288–89). The babbling of politicians and preachers achieves nothing, but "love of land and courage" provokes these Southerners to war against the freedom of that land's slaves (289). Slavery, then, becomes a burden and a test for white people. Ike's version of history is, in fact, a massive denial of white guilt, even though he says that all he wants to find is peace through his explanation of the past. Ike shares with Quentin a suspicion of empty, high-flown rhetoric. Yet like Quentin, he is given to certain verbal extravagances himself.

For Ike as well, the act of putting thoughts into words validates those thoughts. He interrupts Cass, " 'Let me talk now. I'm trying to explain to the head of my family something which I have got to do which I don't quite understand myself, not in justification of it but to explain it if I can' " (288). In asserting his right to speak, as Quentin does with Shreve in *Absalom, Absalom!*, Ike asserts the power of his words. That power is undercut primarily by our recognition of them as justification; Faulkner cannot avoid the burden of white guilt, but reverence for the land so permeates "The Bear" that we recognize Ike in that narration as well. Ike's words establish that his explanation of his repudiation is as vital

as the act of repudiation. Even his discovery in "Delta Autumn"
does not completely negate the value of articulating the chronicle
that explains and makes real Ike's renunciation. In fact, Ike's
words are the interesting, valuable, and hopeful elements in his
repudiation, even in their vulnerability.

Words order Ike McCaslin as much as they do Horace Benbow.
But we see many more of Ike's words and thus become more
involved in the ordering process. Even when his words reveal a
frail logic, they maintain an emotional integrity. They tell the
truth of his heart, and we learn it in the same way that Ike learns
why Cass read "Ode on a Grecian Urn" to him on that day, seven
years earlier, when he could not shoot Old Ben. Again Keats' poem
is for Faulkner the metaphor for the desire to preserve a moment
that cannot ever happen. In this instance, the thing that Ike wants
to preserve, the significance of his relinquished patrimony, is too
ravaged by its history and too weakened by his own racism to
survive. He also is unwilling to accept Cass' interpretation. When
Ike fails to see what the poet's extravagances about a girl have to
do with him, Cass says: " 'He had to talk about something. . . .
He was talking about truth. Truth is one. It doesn't change. It
covers all things which touch the heart—honor and pride and pity
and justice and courage and love' " (297). Seven years ago, Ike
remembers, he thought it had to have been simpler than Cass
explained it, and now in the present, Ike still wants life to be
simple. By refusing the land of his fathers, by explaining its history, Ike believes he can stop the racial conflicts that have torn
the land apart.[8] The specific situation, Ike's decision to repudiate
his birthright, illustrates the larger truth behind it. Ike McCaslin
wants to believe that he can preserve his idea of the wilderness
and that he can stop his family's history of miscegenation by
detailing its history and then declaring the end of the trauma.
Language is the means by which people make the world compre-
hensible, and that understanding *is* the truth, according to Ike.

Faulkner also appears to believe strongly in the word's power
to reveal truth. Abstract words like *freedom* and *humility* and
pride provide the connection between Old Ben and black people,
both of whom Ike at least believes have been ennobled by suffer-

ing.[9] Keats too relies on words like *truth* and *beauty* to touch his readers' hearts. The application of specifics becomes a matter for the individual heart. Just before Ike recalls Cass' reading to him, he thinks of how Lion taught him to understand the paradox of humility and pride. It is a simple lesson. Its narration illustrates the rhetorical habit of avoiding any word too specific to have general application, while at the same time, approaching the "true" definition. This technique is evident in the description of Lion:

> A little dog . . . who couldn't be dangerous because there was nothing anywhere much smaller, not fierce because that would have been called just noise, not humble because it was already too near the ground to genuflect, and not proud because it would not have been close enough for anyone to discern what was casting that shadow. (296)

This passage appears just after we learn that Sam Fathers could not have defined the "humility and pride" that Ike McCaslin must learn from him and the dog. The essence of the two, paradoxically paired qualities seems beyond the capacity of words to describe it. The dog is what can only be suggested and not named, but in the recitation of the qualities he cannot possess, we witness the subtle revision of our common definitions of them. The qualities themselves undergo redefinition as we contrast the material restrictions that are often placed on them with the suggested, truer definitions. In a brilliant turnabout, the narrator suggests that the dog does possess the best of humility, for example, because he cannot partake of the human tendency toward false, mechanical humility. The word is redefined, or reinfused with meaning through negation.

Many critics have noted Faulkner's affinity for Keats' poem, but I think Canfield makes a central point when he discusses its inclusion in "The Bear" as the transient expression of Ike's futile desire for transcendence. Certainly Ike wants a finer, truer communication beyond words, but Ike also knows that words are all he has to get him to that definable region of the human heart. And while words do not erase time, death, and hate, they can transcend them for a time when they touch the heart. Horace Benbow apologetically believes that poetry is the closest that we can come to suggesting and understanding truth; Ike and his cousin practice that belief with conviction.

Yet Ike's words ultimately change nothing in the world. His declaration of freedom appears to be false. But it is also false to relegate all he has said to the same category as that of the empty babble of politicians and preachers. Dealing in absolutes is dangerous. Perhaps at the end, Uncle Ike discovers the ambivalence in his own heart when he has to face his "amazement, pity, and outrage" (361) at the mulatto's presence. Not only did the McCaslin family history continue, but for Ike the idea of miscegenation still holds the same trauma. His advice to her, " 'Go back North. Marry: a man in your own race' " (363), makes clear to us that Ike has transcended nothing.[10] He perhaps learns that it was not enough to declare fifty years ago that "Sam Fathers set me free" (301) and have it be true. Or perhaps in wanting to declare the whole land free as well, Ike tries to memorialize the mythic American wilderness that now bears the scars of mechanized progress.[11] The stories of Major de Spain and Sam Fathers have risen, in his mind, "into a dimension free of both time and space . . . where the wild strong immortal game ran forever before the tireless belling immortal hounds, falling and rising phoenix-like to the soundless guns" (354). Words remembered in silence, enlarging and fixing experience, are again the end point. After the woman leaves Ike's tent, we are told that "once again the tent held only silence and the sound of rain. And cold too" (364). Ike remains in a cold quiet similar to that which Quentin comes to as the story of Sutpen reaches its end. The difference between the silence that Ike's imagination creates and the one that he lies in, rigid and shaking, is significantly large. That gap also appears to deal a powerful blow to Ike's faith in the word to make a difference in the world.

Yet the words of the young woman, not remembered stories, trigger the silence in which Ike finally recognizes the limits of his version of history. She reminds him of the love between blacks and whites that so terrifies him he can only hope to stop it by explaining why it will never work. By giving Ike the final word in "Delta Autumn," Faulkner gives us reason to believe Ike understands the defeat of his earlier words; at the same time, he opens the possibility that in Ike's understanding lies some hope of healing the legacy of racial divisions. By naming the deer that Roth Edmonds shot, "It was a doe" (365), Ike voices the treachery in the human heart. His words can be a declaration of doom, a warning, an admission of defeat, or an indication of cleared vision, but the ambiguity is certainly a call to keep the possibilities for language open. The problem is that Faulkner is unsure of what will or can come next.

Ike, of course, does not have the last word in the book. He is not the only narrator nor is he simply Faulkner's mouthpiece. Nevertheless there are strong connections among Ike's efforts to tell his family's history, Gavin's Old Testament project, and Faulkner's writing of *Go Down, Moses*.[12] The fact that Faulkner spends much of his writing career tracing and piecing together strands of the past is not a new observation, but a closer look at the language and construction of this book reveals Faulkner's yearnings not only to achieve origins but to achieve God-like authority.

In its language and subject, *Go Down, Moses* reveals that Faulkner saw himself and his country as positioned before an uncertain and disturbing future. We know that in 1940 he was worried about making a difference in a world that he felt was increasingly threatened and threatening. We also know that he was having trouble writing, an even more immediate threat to achieving immortality. That he was also reading *Moby Dick* to his daughter at this time makes it even more probable that *Go Down, Moses* is, in part, the result of its author's desire to write the words that would explain and even save America.[13] The biographical details simply reinforce what the book itself sets forth: the story of America's land and people must be chronicled so that readers might understand the deep racial divisions that scar both. Just as the mythic hunt in the romantic wilderness was supposed to bring Ike McCaslin to manhood, the writing of the mythic American book seems to be Faulkner's mark against time and change.[14]

Faulkner takes the connections he makes between his writing and the Bible more seriously in *Go Down, Moses* than he does in any preceding novel. His power as an author is at issue now in

ways it never has been before. Biblical allusions start with the
title: in Exodus 19:21 God tells Moses to "Go down" and to take
the Ten Commandments to the people. The Commandments are
the ultimate authoritative discourse, in Bakhtinian terms, but *Go
Down, Moses* maintains an uneasy balance between aspiring to be
the Sacred Writ and retelling the old stories in new words. The
title also alludes to the Negro spiritual, a significant recasting of
the white man's words. But the triumph in the song's final words
stands in implicit condemnation of whites' repeated attempts to
"Let [these] people go."[15] Historically, freedom has been a gift and
not a right for black people. Implicit in the very idea of Ike's
repudiation is evidence of the novel's inescapable connections to
white paternalism. Isaac McCaslin is both the same as and different from Isaac the son of Abraham: " 'born into a later life than
Abraham's and repudiating immolation: fatherless and therefore
safe declining the altar because maybe this time the exasperated
Hand might not supply the kid' " (283). In Ike's version, Isaac
becomes Abraham, a fitting retelling in a book in which no son can
escape the sins of his fathers.

Ike's repudiation makes no one safe, but the issue of patrimony
is nevertheless taken seriously, particularly by Ike and Lucas
Beauchamp. Faulkner holds to the belief that names as well as
blood will tell. It is fitting that he takes the name for his leading
character from the one of Abraham's sons that God recognized and
in whom he established his covenant (Genesis 17:19). Melville had
already rewritten the story of Ishmael, the son of Abraham and
Hagar, the Egyptian bondwoman. The Old Testament Isaac's racial purity is a rewritten detail that underscores the lie in Ike's
presumed entitlement, one that comes not just from his paternity
but also from his race. When Ike realizes by reading the ledgers
that Lucas has changed his name from Lucius, he reminds us again
of his faith in the power of the word:

> [Lucas] simply eliminated the word from the name; not denying,
> declining the name itself, because he used three quarters of it; but
> simply taking the name and changing it, altering it, making it no
> longer the white man's but his own, by himself composed, himself

self-progenitive and nominate, by himself ancestored, as, for all the old ledgers recorded to the contrary, old Carothers himself was. (281)

Lucas' strength and pride, most powerful when he and Zack Edmonds fight in "The Fire and the Hearth," is also the point of the name change. Although Lucas' effort to free himself is no more successful than Ike's, the act of naming himself, if only partially, is not empty. Ike grants him a dignity that comes out of respect for the man, not simply his "white" blood. But Ike's words also reveal his reverence for the idea of self creation even as they connect Lucas to old Carothers, the white father who started it all. But no more than Ike, can Lucas Beauchamp escape the old fears and hatreds that gave him McCaslin blood and then forced him to endure the white man's indignities: " 'How to God can a black man ask a white man to please not lay down with his black wife?' " (59). His second question, " 'And even if he could ask it, how to God can the white man promise he wont?,' " frames the sense of inevitability against which the characters and Faulkner struggle. The belief in the power of history and blood to determine the present and future paradoxically challenges and reinforces the power of the word. Sam Fathers' father, Ikkemotubbe, names himself "Doom" and has a son with a quadroon slave woman. The prophetic naming reiterates Faulkner's belief in words; it is powerfully accurate, but it also signifies the hopelessness that threatens the power of any word or act to effect change.

Thus long after Doom is dead, the tragedies of miscegenation and racism continue. Lucas' pride, epitomized in his self-naming, and Ike's renunciation " 'Sam Fathers set me free,' " are so central to Faulkner's role as author and so tied to the racial conflict that they echo in all the words of *Go Down, Moses*. Faulkner not only knew well the need to have his words make a difference but also the fear that the problem was too large for any words to define. The telling is loaded with white guilt and grief and with the writer's complicated expectations for its power to expiate them. Gavin and particularly Ike set about to deal with Faulkner's version of white people's burden in ways that reinforce the author's connections to his characters. Gavin's Old Testament project is mentioned to emphasize his ineffectiveness, but the book attempts the same kind of return to origins. Like the Bible, Faulkner's book depends heavily on documentation and parable to explain present-day conflict. And Ike's effort to understand by narrating his family's history mirrors Faulkner's method.

The book opens with a tribute to history. "Was" introduces us to Ike the old man and then moves into the past to begin to explain why this childless widower has refused the land of his birthright. Then "The Fire and the Hearth" juxtaposes Lucas' ridiculously stubborn struggle with Roth for gold with the dramatic and moving fight he has forty years earlier with Zack over his taking Mollie for his son's wet nurse and perhaps for his mistress. In the present all of these characters appear diminished, worn,[16] except for Rider in "Pantaloon in Black" and Mollie Beauchamp in "Go Down, Moses." Their voices, even filtered through a white writer's imagination, speak eloquently but too briefly of the painful gulf between black reality and white perception of it. The sheriff's self-righteous outrage at Rider's behavior after his wife dies is an irony that powerfully accents the white man's limitations. The sheriff sees blacks as the other but not as humans: " 'When it comes to the normal human feelings and sentiments . . . they might just as well be a damn herd of wild buffaloes' " (154). A more subtle, more insidious form of making the black person strange is Gavin Stevens' handling of Mollie's requests with a detached irony that condescends to her grief and pride. "Go Down, Moses" lacks the power of "Pantaloon in Black," in part because the narrator adopts the same faintly condescending attitude that Gavin has. In this description of Miss Worsham, Mollie, the editor, and Gavin, the narrator's Latinate flourishes mock Samuel Worsham Beauchamp's ignominious end: "the high-headed erect white woman, the old Negress, the designated paladin of justice and truth, and right, the Heidleberg Ph.D.—in formal component complement to the Negro murderer's catafalque: the slain wolf" (382). Critical consensus is that "Go Down, Moses" in general and Gavin's clear relief to get back to the business of his life make for a weak denouement. The present is a mundane, almost incomprehending continuation of the past's racial agonies. Telling seems to have made little difference; it doesn't help Faulkner find a way out.

But *Go Down, Moses* is no failure. Faulkner does write an important history of a particularly painful part of America's past. Although he sets the story inside a specific family in the South, Faulkner works continually to make it not just Southern but American. And then he casts America's legacy of racial conflict in mythic proportions. The problem that Faulkner confronts directly in the section "Go Down, Moses" is that his history of America cannot represent the voice it agonizes over. Critics have long discussed the ways that Faulkner and Ike mythologize the wilderness and the ritual hunt.[17] The language of "The Old People" and "The Bear" consciously moves the woods, Old Ben, and his pursuers backward into time and upward into mythic transcendence. In these sections, Faulkner most clearly identifies himself with Ike's desire to uncover and immortalize the truths of the human heart that will explain its treachery and grief. Ike and Sam Fathers are "the white boy, marked forever, and the old dark man sired on both sides by savage kings" (165), a description that makes them more than individuals and underlines the sense of timelessness that infuses the narrative. The difference between this description and the one of the "complement to the Negro murderer's catafalque" is a telling indication of the gulf between Faulkner and the black consciousness he seeks to understand. Part of the reason for that gulf lies in the description of the "white" Ike and the "dark" Sam. Thinking in terms of color is not just the problem; it appears impossible to escape. The language in these center stories is particularly weighted with heavily qualified, self-conscious, yet actually majestic sentences that keep us aware of the import of their subject. Insofar as he sets forth white America's history, weaving together its tangled strands of entitlement and guilt, respect and disregard for nature and God, Faulkner is convincing in his authority.

Another part of the truth that *Go Down, Moses* tells is that the shadow of miscegenation and racism is long and perhaps permanent. The old Ike of "Delta Autumn" experiences this truth in the

cold and decidedly unmajestic present. Faulkner knows the threat
of Ike's discovery. It leaves him unable to bring the authority with
which he chronicles the past into the present. The desire for
authority endangers his ability to hear the other and perhaps to
find a way out of the trap of racial conflict.

5

The Language of Responsibility

The writer has a very great responsibility. The writer is the person that will record man's endeavor . . . The writer's responsibility is to tell the truth in such a way that it will be memorable, that people will read it, will remember it because it was told in some memorable way. . . . he has got to take the truth and set it on fire so that people will remember it.—Faulkner in *Lion in the Garden*

Many times in the last twelve years of his life, William Faulkner spoke publicly about writing and about his concern for humanity's survival. The connection between the two subjects was, for him, absolute. Beginning with his Nobel address in 1950, Faulkner took the public occasion as an opportunity to define the writer's role in the world: "The poet's voice need not merely be the record of man, it can be one of the props, the pillars to help him endure."[1] Although Faulkner probably uses the word *poet* to mean *writer*, the metonym reminds us of the poet's favored status in his imagination. And in Faulkner's later novels it makes increasing sense to bear in mind Bakhtin's distinction between the language of poetry and the novel. Bakhtin's idea of poetic language adds an important dimension to the body of critical explanation for the growing preoccupation in the late work with setting forth the truth of "man's endeavor." Bakhtin suggests, "The language in a poetic work realizes itself as something about which there can

119

be no doubt, something that cannot be disputed, something all-encompassing" ("Discourse in the Novel," 286).

In the latter half of his career, Faulkner's achievement as a novelist was more troubled than energized by his desire to encompass all, to have his words stand free of the altering presence of the other. He is not a "failed poet" but a novelist who struggles with the lure of the absolute word. But now Faulkner struggles as well to make his personal vision a public one. Never fully comfortable with public attention, Faulkner nevertheless appears to have taken his responsibility seriously. He addressed an international audience. Students recorded his every response; even the State Department requested his participation in several writers' conferences to promote America's good will.[2] Each time he spoke of the writer's responsibility, Faulkner strengthened the connection between language and the survival of humanity, and his career as a literary statesman bears out the strong moral overtones of his later novels. It also testifies to the direction that his lifelong concerns about language had taken him. The words he spoke and the words he wrote during this time were freighted with his belief that the writer must set the truth on fire.[3] Dialogic explorations of the possibilities in language give way to a new urgency to enlighten and to change humanity through the word. His belief in telling the truth in "some memorable way" identifies the writer as both the possessor and disseminator of the truth. When asked by a Japanese translator about the intricacies of his style, Faulkner explained it in terms of personal need: "In my own case anyway, it's the compulsion to say everything in one sentence because you may not live long enough to have two sentences."[4] That concern, coupled with the responsibility of his task, creates an exigency that resonates in all of the novels that follow *Go Down, Moses*.

Of those novels, all but *A Fable* (1954) and *The Reivers* (1962) feature Gavin Stevens. To revive a character whose presence in *Light in August* and *Go Down, Moses* is not only minor but essentially negative, and then to give him a sizable and increasingly positive role appears whimsical, if not contradictory. But as the last in Faulkner's career-long line of "men of words," Gavin makes perfect sense. Gavin Stevens is not William Faulkner, but like his predecessors, he stands as the fictional embodiment of the anxieties and desires that inform Faulkner's writing life.

Gavin is a middle-aged leader in the Jefferson community, and while acutely aware of his own foibles, he serves as commentator on humanity's. In the novels after *Go Down, Moses*, Faulkner exhibits greater interest in similar commentary and summary. He completes the Snopes saga in *The Town* (1957) and *The Mansion* (1959); he chronicles Southern history in *Intruder in the Dust* (1948) and *Requiem for a Nun* (1951), and he alludes to and even retells parts from several earlier works in the final chapter of *The Mansion*.[5] Gavin has a significant role in each of these novels. He appears as well in some of the detective stories in *Knight's Gambit* (1949). None of these books achieve the brilliance of *Absalom, Absalom!* or *Light in August*, but as they round out Faulkner's career, they tell us a great deal about the sense of writing against time that informs each. The four later novels in which Gavin appears are connected by Faulkner's assertion of authority as the recorder of social history. Although Gavin is not a character in *A Fable*, I have included it in this discussion because it is a large-scale execution of the authority Faulkner asserts in his other works. That it is also perhaps his biggest failure is absolutely part of the point. I have not included *The Reivers* because, although it is more successful than *A Fable*, it is a retrospective that otherwise adds little to my reading of the demands Faulkner, at this point in his career, made of his writing. *Go Down, Moses* ends in a present that only emphasizes the old and still unbridged gulf between whites and blacks. As Gavin Stevens turns to his desk and away from the disturbing implications of Mollie Beauchamp's presence, Faulkner reaches the limits of his own capacity to understand and to imagine the black consciousness, and thus to write the black voice. As I have argued earlier, Faulkner's black characters, as well as his women, show us the limitations of a language that acknowledges the presence of the other. Because the female and black characters are radically different from their author, they allow us to see them more clearly as projections of a single consciousness. Faulkner's best writing has always cultivated the tension between the word and a response to it; now the response, or the other, is more difficult to conjure. The issue of race does not disappear from the fiction, nor does Faulkner's awareness of the multivoiced world. But now Faulkner turns to his desk and writes with a greater determination to write his own voice. Faulkner's conception of himself as writer is embedded in the recurring figure of Jefferson's genial lawyer.

One constant characterizes Gavin's roles as lawyer, uncle, friend, and narrator—he is an explainer. Gavin talks a great deal. At times, he is verbose and tedious, but most often he communicates skillfully to the reader and to other characters. His education has not limited him to a Latinate, elitist lexicon; he knows enough about the power of language to speak in the vernacular whenever necessary. In a short story, "Tomorrow," from *Knight's Gambit*, Gavin's nephew Chick Mallison, observes that his uncle could "talk so that all the people in our country—the Negroes, the hill people, the rich flatland plantations owners—understood what he said."[6] With unwitting condescension, Faulkner locates plurality in one mouthpiece. Gavin's verbal skill gives him as much authority as his law degree does—to be able to speak everyone's language is to gain credence and thus the power to persuade. In *Intruder in the Dust*, the only way Gavin can get Lucas Beauchamp to tell him how he managed to land in jail is to speak to him sternly, as to a child—and in his own dialect. In the same novel, Gavin helps to bring the adolescent Chick to terms with the South's legacy of racial prejudice by telling him its history. In doing so, he presents the white Southerner's justification for separatism that echoes Faulkner's public statements about segregation.[7] In *Requiem for a Nun*, Gavin talks *for* Temple Drake during their interview with the governor. Speaking both as a lawyer and as her friend, Gavin negotiates legal procedure and language, asks questions to determine events, and finally takes over Temple's testimony, presenting his words as hers. In *The Town*, Gavin shares narrative responsibility with his nephew and Ratliff, and, as narrator, Gavin works to persuade an unknown audience of certain truths about the Snopes clan and about human nature. He shares the desire to turn experience into words with Horace and the others, but Faulkner gives Gavin more power and a greater range by underscoring his reliability. When Gavin recounts the Snopes' saga, he adopts the chatty informative tone of one explaining something to a friend. Sometimes he talks directly to the reader: " 'Farming?' I said (all right, cried if you like.)"[8] The effect is to pull the reader more intimately into a story that Gavin is quickly making his. Gavin's concern for the right word is an author's concern, and his role in *The Town* is that of storyteller. As narrator, he summarizes action, draws conclusions, and provides a rationale for action; he makes meaning out of a mixture of fact and conjecture.

It is also through the narrative that Gavin gains a certain control over the Snopeses. Part of his control comes from the sardonic tone in which he relates many of the Snopeses' activities. Wit creates a distance that allows him a position of superiority, as when he consoles Ratliff about the loss of Flem Snopes' share in a local restaurant: " 'What else are we going to do about them [but laugh]? Of course you've got the best joke: you dont have to fry hamburgers any more. But give them time; maybe they got one taking a correspondence-school law course. Then I wont have to be acting city attorney any more either' " (*Town*, 44). But humor is only one method of verbal control that Gavin employs against the villainy of Flem Snopes. By giving voice to his interpretation of Flem's motives, Gavin asserts a kind of power over him. The entire town of Jefferson seems helpless in the face of Flem's gradual but absolute control over their lives. Gavin makes Flem more concrete and thus less fearful by explaining him. Gavin's words make Flem Snopes a known quantity.

There is strength in knowing the enemy, and for Gavin, Flem is a personal enemy as well as a civic menace. He explains that Eula Varner can never be called Eula Snopes, even though he knows that she and Flem are married, because "it must not simply because I would decline to have it so" (*Town*, 132). In calling Eula by her maiden name, Gavin robs Flem Snopes of any real connection to her. For Gavin, names establish order and make feelings real. His belief in the power of names is also an explicit part of his narration. Reflecting on the unhappy coincidence that Byron Snopes now works at the Sartoris bank and that the "original" Snopes had been a member of old Colonel Sartoris' calvary unit during the Civil War, Gavin says, "The horse which at last came home to roost sounded better. Not witty, but rather an immediate unified irrevocably scornful front to what the word Snopes was to mean to us, and to all others, no matter who, whom simple juxtaposition to the word irrevocably smirched and contaminated" (43).

Gavin's words do more than reiterate his sense of their power; they also underscore his unease with the contamination to the proud old heritage that the Snopes signify. For all the qualifications he puts upon that heritage, Faulkner essentially resists the free enterprise system's threat to the old plantation system. Flem Snopes is dangerous to an entire way of life. He is the other, the outsider who threatens change. The issue, at base, is power. Faulkner recognizes all human relations as systems of exchange, and that directly informs his awareness of language as a system of exchange. But just as Jefferson struggles against Flem Snopes' encroachment, Gavin struggles to assert the authority of his words. Faulkner gives him a great deal of power to do so. In the course of Gavin's defense of Southern separatism in *Intruder*, he justifies the system in terms of a concept that threatens more than just the sense of his argument:

> Only a few of us know that only from homogeneity comes anything of a people or for a people of durable and lasting value—the literature, the art, the science . . . And as for Lucas Beauchamp, Sambo, he's a homogeneous man too, except that part of him which is trying to escape not even into the best of the white race.[9]

As bizarre and painful as this passage is, it bears examination. First, for a man who believes in the power of names, Gavin shows remarkable insensitivity in calling Lucas "Sambo." Beyond that, the idea of homogeneity not so subtly serves as defensive justification for racist thinking and for closing off a novel from any real threat of the responding other. As Myra Jehlen points out, the basic assumption in *Intruder* is that the white definition of black and the white definition of Southern history are universal truths.[10] The plot as well as the exchanges between Gavin and Chick reinforce the perspective, however well intentioned, that the black race is to be defined and ultimately set free by whites. When on the ride to Caledonia Chapel Chick notices the absence of black sharecroppers, he thinks of them as "the land's living symbol . . . the beast the plow and the man" (147) and thus underscores the way in which black people are given meaning by white people. However dignified Lucas Beauchamp is, he still remains passive and removed from the central action and concern of the novel: what it means to whites to set free the black race. Even though Gavin recognizes the irony and immorality in the continuing need to enact this gesture, he ultimately defends the white race's need, if not right, to do so. The authority in Gavin's words is borne out by the novel's conclusion. Chick is integrated into the system that keeps blacks separate and mysterious, and Lucas' proud and dignified acquiescence to Gavin's token bill, as well as his request for a receipt, ties the entire monologue into a neat, closed package. The effect of this is to make us aware that the novel is closed off from the black voice it seeks to represent. Darwin Turner makes this point clear when he observes that the "moralistic, idealistic, but naive Faulkner fails to consider [that] . . . blacks are just as anxious as the white Thomas Sutpens to realize their goals within their own lifetimes" and that white praise of black endurance and dignity under conditions whites have imposed deflects attention from the real issue—white people have a difficult time even realizing that they need to listen to the black voice.[11] I think Faulkner knew some of that; his preoccupation with the other in language would make it difficult to avoid. But the issue also points up the difficulty all people have in getting outside their own perspectives, and for my purposes, Faulkner's, in giving over the power he could claim for in his own words.

Faulkner does, however, ask us to question Gavin's power. The challenge comes less from the responses of others than from Gavin himself. In *Intruder in the Dust*, we learn something of what Gavin has taught his nephew about language: "[Chick] remembered his uncle saying once how little of vocabulary man really needed to get comfortably and even efficiently through his life, how not only in the individual but within his whole type and race and kind a few simple cliches served his few simple passions and needs and lusts"

(48). Given Gavin's own loquaciousness, this observation appears to be either very condescending or evidence of real confusion. It also demonstrates the way that language allows Gavin to set himself apart as a commentator on human behavior, much as Horace, Darl, and Ike do. Implicit in the remark is an awareness of a disjunction between life and talking, or writing, about life. Gavin too cannot entirely accept language as a system of exchange, but the consequences are much less threatening for him.

Gavin is made foolish and ineffectual at times when Faulkner connects the character's affinity for words to his timidity, particularly concerning women. In the tortured tradition of Horace and Quentin, Gavin has real trouble with real-life women. Once again, language is implicated directly as Gavin's narrative, especially in *The Town*, is riddled with his defensive justifications of his relation to Eula's daughter, Linda. The entire involvement is charged with his intense but unrequited love for Eula. When he contacts Linda through a series of notes (because notes allow him a distance the telephone does not), we see the painful worry and fastidious attention he gives every elaborately casual phrase. Gavin's behavior toward Linda is always correct and avuncular, but in his story of his efforts to help Linda leave Jefferson, we see a man trying to come to terms with the passionate force of his feelings and his acute awareness that he has never acted on them.

As he does with Horace, Faulkner turns to T. S. Eliot's Prufrock to highlight Gavin's compulsion to explain himself. In one of several allusions, Gavin describes the time before meeting with Linda as "filled with a thousand indecisions" (206). An important and painful part of Gavin's character is embodied in his self-consciousness:

> *What more can you want of me that I have already failed to do?* But there would be plenty of time for that, I would have plenty of time to eat the sardines and crackers and say What a shame to the account of whatever the recent outrage the President and his party had contrived against Mr Garraway. (*Town*, 313)

The connection Gavin makes between himself and one of poetry's best-known failures both informs his character and validates the language of metaphor and allusion. Gavin sees his problem as one of failing "to do"—his inaction has left him with only tortured introspection. When he tries to fight Manfred de Spain, Gavin realizes he cannot hurt him; he can only try in vain to defend Eula's honor. Gavin is trapped inside his own thoughts and his own words, but paradoxically, these words allow him a means of self-definition, explanation, and thus a kind of control over his situation. The allusion to Prufrock exemplifies the paradox: the meaning appears to be that words fail to make connections between two people, but the vehicle (words) conveys the point with poignant accuracy and thus works to undercut it.

Gavin defines poetry in *Intruder* as "a poet's extravagance which as quite often mirrors truth but upside down and backward since the mirror's unwitting manipulator busy in his preoccupation has forgotten that the back of it is glass too" (195). The mirror is poetry, more specifically, language, and while it comes closest of any of our endeavors to telling the truth, it is not the same as truth. Gavin's "unwitting manipulator" is a more positive version of Horace's puny liar, but both acknowledge that language can obscure as often as it reveals. In this passage as well, Gavin refers to the fallibility of the writer. The back of the mirror is glass, or a transparent window to truth, but the writer can become so involved with words that he forgets how simple the truth is.

Gavin is also acutely aware that words can protect memory. His anxiety over the word's dual function as the preserver of memory and as a reminder of the loss it attempts to recover echoes the anguish of Quentin Compson:

> That was it: the very words *reputation* and *good name*. Merely to say them, give their existence vocal recognition, would irrevocably soil and besmirch them, would destroy the immunity of the very things they represented, leaving them not just vulnerable but already doomed; from the inviolable and proud integrity of principles they would become, reduce to, the ephemeral and already doomed and damned fragility of human conditions; innocence and virginity become symbol and postulant of loss and grief, evermore to be mourned, existing only in the past tense *was* and *now is not, no more nor more*. (*Town*, 202)

Gavin is also so sensitive to the disjunction between the word and meaning, or real and ideal, that just giving the above words *voice* yanks them rudely from sanctity into the temporary, tainted human realm. His words reveal the conflict between his fundamental resistance to change and his awareness that, once uttered or written, his words are no longer his and their meaning is thus susceptible to alteration. On some level, he believes that the word is its meaning, until human voices wrench the two apart; thus saying *virginity* is a form of deflowering. In this passage Gavin mourns the loss of the ideal, which ceases to exist except in the past tense once it is given reality.

It is no accident that Gavin's anxiety about language concerns tense and thus time. His use of the word *irrevocably* in the above passage is significant because it indicates the kind of absolutes for which Gavin yearns. He wishes for and believes in the existence of the ideal—a one, an absolute. At times, such as in this excerpt from *Intruder, the all* is related to time: "yesterday today and tomorrow are Is: Indivisible; One . . . It's all *now* you see. Yesterday wont be over until tomorrow and tomorrow began ten thousand years ago" (194). The existence of the "inviolable and proud integrity of principles" also suggests the all. Ike McCaslin's futile yearning for complete unity is repeated in Gavin Stevens. The desire becomes a preoccupation Faulkner cannot abandon.

In another passage from *The Town*, Gavin struggles to articulate how time becomes inviolable:

> Not *not been*, but rather no more *is*, since *was* remains always and forever, inexplicable and immune, which is its grief. That's what I mean: a dimension less, then the sound of a door and then, not *never been* but simply *no more is* since always and forever that *was* remains as if what is going to happen to one tomorrow already gleams faintly visible now if the watcher were only wise enough to discern it or maybe just brave enough. (334)

By making nouns into verbs, Gavin retains some control. He turns words that describe transitory states of being into presences, ideas. Gavin articulates the paradox of language that troubles Faulkner as well. *Was* remains forever—an absolute that cannot be changed—and this is grievous because our instinct is to act, to rectify. Yet in the very act of *remaining*, the past retains the power to exert its influence. The persistence of memory may be painful to Gavin here, but it implies another kind of immunity that can offer great power. The original moment is gone, but its memory and the words that give it reality remain. Language may be unable to recover one loss, but it keeps the presence of that loss alive. Finally Gavin connects his acute sense of loss to the future, as if even acknowledgement of the past carries with it a stubborn refusal to grant it complete immutability. He speaks of a connection between past, present, and future, of life as one very large unit or cycle. Memory binds the past to the present and the cycle binds both to the future. In that notion lies the hope that we can affect tomorrow, if we are brave enough to trust what we know of yesterday and today. In *Requiem for a Nun*, Gavin tells Temple Drake that " 'the past is never dead. It's not even past.' "[12] Faulkner asserts the truth of Gavin's words in every book he wrote.

Again Faulkner centers Gavin's struggle around living with the threats that time, other words, and the approximate nature of language itself pose to his own words. If this is true, then what assurance can we have that we can ever really know or preserve anything? When Gavin regrets his inability to deal in even a quasi-businesslike manner with Eula, he describes his regret in terms of language: "And goodbye. The sad word, even over the telephone. I mean, not the word is sad or the meaning of it, but that you can really say it without grief and anguish not but without even the memory of grief and anguish" (*Town*, 214). Gavin mourns the loss of feeling originally attached to a word. He does not want anything to change, and the fact that he can utter a word without a great deal of feeling means that he cannot preserve *anything*. Again he demonstrates the yearning he shares with the others for absolutes. But Gavin does not just long for absolutes, he believes in them. He also knows that change (in feelings and thus in the meaning of the words that express feelings) exists. Change threatens his belief in absolutes, and so he spends most of his time trying to disprove his fear that he cannot reach and preserve anything.

Gavin's unease about language's approximate nature explains

his translation project. Mentioned again in *The Mansion* as a kind of druglike escape, Gavin's plan is to translate the Old Testament first into classical Greek and then into Hebrew "and really attain to purity."[13] Gavin's motive is to seek origins; his methodical approach indicates a belief that purity can be attained logically and through language. It is no accident that he is working with "the Word of God." The notion that oneness or purity can be attained through language links Gavin to the seventeenth-century desire to establish a universal grammar. Behind these efforts was the belief that language is a picture of a high-ordered universe, and that writing could create a universe to match God's nature.[14] In *Intruder in the Dust*, Gavin's nephew connects the Eucharist with the kind of unity Gavin is seeking: "the deathless blood of our Lord not to be tasted, moving not downward toward the stomach but upward and outward into the Allknowledge between good and evil and the choice and the repudiation and the acceptance forever" (100). Already Chick Mallison understands that the wine he sips at church symbolizes something even larger than the blood of Christ. The "Allknowledge" seems to be what Gavin is reaching for when he declares that the past, present, and future exist together, or when he endeavors to translate the Bible back into the language of its origin.

But Faulkner appears to stand aside and shake his head at Gavin's aspirations, and of course the project is never completed. In fact, Gavin relinquishes it finally when his love for Linda causes him to make himself an accomplice in the murder of Flem Snopes. He defies every moral and legal principle he has upheld all his life for an amorphous world in which "there aren't any morals. . . . people just do the best they can" (*Mansion*, 429). Gavin's relinquishment comes at the end of the last novel in which he appears, so it would seem that Faulkner is pushing for a resolution. Gavin's words do not endorse amorality, nor are they nihilistic. Instead he seems to accept the limits of our ability to reach the ideal, without denying its existence at all. Implicit in his words is the acceptance that man-made moral codes and laws may not reflect a higher law. He wants to believe in a moral, ordered universe, and he wants to believe in the authority and sanctity of the words that compose the order. Gavin's pronouncement carries authority because it is tempered with his recognition that all people are connected in the struggle to negotiate the things they cannot control.[15] Words make that connection; they are the way he can communicate to himself, and to Ratliff, and to us all of the telling, explaining, conjecturing, and justifying that is as necessary to his life as breathing. It is precisely because language is so important that Gavin is acutely aware of the problems it causes. In *The Mansion*, he speculates that "perhaps the entire dilemma of man's condition is because of the ceaseless babble with which he has surrounded himself, enclosed himself, insulated himself from the penalties of his own folly, which otherwise—the penalties, the simple red ink—might have enabled him by now to have made his condition solvent, workable, successful" (236). Thus we have Gavin's verbose, yet pertinent, definition of language as excuse-maker. People do hide behind and twist words. Gavin even does a bit of that himself.

The danger in Gavin's desire to insulate himself with his own words, to assert his authority through them is nowhere clearer than in his relations with women. Gavin possesses the stereotypic ideas about women that all of Faulkner's men share. The irony is that Gavin's problems with women are exactly his problems with language. In his yearning for the absolute ideal, he closes himself and his words off from the far more complicated response of the other. When Gavin first sees Eula, after several years' deprivation, he remarks on how small she seems. For the reader, Eula becomes remarkably less goddesslike in *The Town* as soon as she speaks. Described in *The Hamlet* as the "supreme primal uterus" and the object of Gavin's purest love, she becomes surprisingly human when she talks. Gavin himself remarks on this in *The Mansion* when he explains the difference between Helen and all the other beauties of history: "Helen was light . . . (the others were) not like Helen. . . . It's because the others all talked. They are fading steadily into the obscurity of their own vocality within which their passions and tragedies took place" (133). In the same novel, Chick Mallison comments on his uncle's growing love for Linda Snopes, now a deaf widow, in terms of her enforced silence:

That was it: silence. If there were no such thing as sound. If it only took place in silence, no evil man has invented could really harm him: explosion, treachery, the human voice.
That was it: deafness . . . immobilized by a thunderclap into silence . . . the inviolate bride of silence, inviolable in maidenhead, fixed, forever safe from change and alteration. (203)

Although Chick, not Gavin, speaks here, he focuses on the exact idea that has always plagued his uncle. In addition, his paraphrase of the opening line of "Ode on a Grecian Urn" reminds us of the same need to preserve the idea of female purity in words that Faulkner gives to Horace Benbow and Quentin Compson and Joe Christmas. It torments their lives far more completely than it does Gavin's, however. Gavin also associates silence with purity and with an absolute, permanent safety, but while talking makes the other women obscure, Gavin's language makes Helen unique. And it is Gavin who first gives Linda a pad and a pencil, so "everybody could hear." Both passages underscore Gavin's desire for the ideal and makes the connection between the ideal and language explicit. As long as Gavin can write about or explain the ideal, he can keep it ideal. As soon as the ideal takes part in the communication, she threatens his version. He no longer has control. Gavin is aware of this, and Faulkner makes him a bit ineffectual at times, but in general, Gavin retains a good deal of control. Although neither he nor Faulkner sees it, the persistent belief that women, children, and all black people have an uncomplicated dignity and are closer to truth than white males is a condescending assertion of power. According to this theory, these simpler beings know truth because they do not talk or think or try to impose order and reason on life. Thus we have Gavin's description of his efforts to introduce Linda Snopes to a college education outside of Mississippi as "corrupting her mind, inserting her mind and her imagination not just the impractical dreamy folly in poetry books but the fatal position of dissatisfaction's hopes and dreams" (*Town*, 285). Although we know that Gavin's dissatisfaction with himself stems from his belief in the poets' "dreamy folly," his words still manage to assert control over Linda. If she stays simple and uneducated, she remains closer to his romantic idea of woman. He may never actually "have" that ideal, but he can at least stay removed from the real-life counterpart. Even when Gavin realizes that he cannot prevent Linda from facilitating Mink's murder of Flem Snopes, he still manages to stand apart and interpret the events.

In the end, Gavin's pain and confusion are only superficially resolved. He denies Ratliff's contention that Linda planned Flem's murder, but he gives Mink Snopes the money she left him. *The Mansion* closes with a sense of resolution because the social exchanges have been completed, scores have been settled, debts paid. Then Mink Snopes lies down on the earth, which speaks to him in his own language, "Come on, lay down; I aint going to hurt you" (434). That the voice is calling Mink back to the anonymity and unity of death is clear, and critics generally agree that Faulkner is summing up not just a novel but a career. The final, very long sentence is itself a "long human recording" (436) that blanks out human distinctions as it moves to transcend them. Gavin summarizes our living, "People just do the best they can," but Faulkner integrates it into a larger pattern.

Gavin's anxieties about the inexact and vulnerable word, his habit of defining behavior, his desire for absolutes give Faulkner a way to write more directly the habits of mind that he knew informed all of his writing.[16] Significantly, Gavin's anxieties about language are less personally tragic and less complicated than those of his predecessors. The need to assert the authority of language meets with far less resistance and, most readers would agree, far less brilliant results. Faulkner's awareness of his own mortality and deep concern about America and the world surely contribute to the language of responsibility that fills the later novels. The dialogic undercurrent of Faulkner's ideas about language does not disappear from these novels, but it does become much less open-ended. The novels are, in general, preoccupied with Faulkner's need to write the world and to save it. In 1944 Faulkner told Malcolm Cowley, "I am telling the same story over and over, which is myself and the world."[17] By 1944 Faulkner was beginning to attach inordinate responsibility to his story, and that necessarily began to revise his idea of language.

The two novels that best illustrate the growing demands that

Faulkner made in his writing are *Requiem for a Nun* and *A Fable*. Although Gavin is only in *Requiem*, his desire for his words to become *the word* lives in both books. In neither does Faulkner achieve the transforming, transcendent work he aspired to. They are too difficult to read, too heavy with moral purpose. Both novels do give extensive testament to his professed compulsion "to say everything in one sentence," a fact that richly complicates his claims for the power of language. At the same time that the novels serve as Faulkner's warning to and hope for humanity, they warn and explain again and again, suggesting some worry over the efficacy of his words.

The novels also contain long passages of powerfully persuasive rhetoric. And although he no longer experiments with the narrative techniques that distinguish many of the earlier novels, Faulkner continues to look for the innovative way to tell his story. With these two novels he stretches the conventional boundaries among genres, making them something more than fiction. *Requiem* is part play, part history, and *A Fable* is a quasi-allegorical discussion of the failure of pacifism that incorporates a tall tale and several digressions into world history. The mixing of usually discrete genres is an assertion of power, Faulkner's declaration that he is beyond the dictates of any one form. In the pattern of Melville, Faulkner alters the traditional novel form by adding to it, a technique consistent with the novel's dialogism. But behind the mixing is also the desire to encompass all. Both *Requiem* and *A Fable* are encyclopedic, but both novels, and particularly *A Fable*, also lack much of the vitality and drama of Faulkner's earlier work. Idea now looms larger than character, and Faulkner's attention to the multivoiced world is redirected toward articulating a single-voiced language. The sense of exploration and of testing possibilities that invigorates novels like *The Sound and the Fury* and *Absalom, Absalom!* is generally absent from these two novels. Faulkner now delivers conclusions. Yet the writing of *Requiem* and *A Fable* evinces more clearly than any others of this period the tremendous investment in the power of language that Faulkner has been writing toward all along.

Faulkner once said that he wrote *A Fable* from "an idea and a hope."[18] The same can be said of *Requiem for a Nun*, for it also concentrates on unfolding certain fundamental truths about the human condition. Central to both works are long dialogues in which one character talks to convince another of certain truths. In *Requiem*, Temple Drake faces in Nancy Mannigoe both her daughter's murderer and her own culpability in the tragedy. A straightforward dialogue with Gavin Stevens focuses her struggle on the issue of responsibility—to self, to others, and to God. *Requiem* moves resolutely toward a full articulation of why we must suffer our own folly. The novel is its author's statement of responsibility—implicit in the writing is Faulkner's belief that it will inform its readers' actions. That faith is more explicitly a part of *A Fable*. Faulkner labored nearly ten years on the novel he considered a tour de force. Beginning with a simple question—what would happen if men just refused to fight?—Faulkner restages World War I. The novel is Faulkner's long and complex answer to why people create wars. It is also his elaborate record of humankind, and perhaps more significantly, it is William Faulkner's "pillar" against human destruction. In a letter explaining the novel to Robert Haas, Faulkner reveals the extent of his hopes for *A Fable:* "I am not trying to preach at all. But that is the argument: We did this in 1918; in 1944 it not only MUST NOT happen again, it SHALL NOT HAPPEN again."[19] Although his rhetoric betrays a definite didacticism, Faulkner seems to have made a distinction, at least in his own mind, between his aversion to sermonizing and his faith in language to deliver truth and to constitute action as a result of that truth. The difference is at times indistinguishable to the readers of *A Fable* and *Requiem*, because the investment he makes in the power of his words places a significantly greater demand upon his language.

In turn, the demands that Faulkner makes upon the reader change. By giving his words the total responsibility to delineate human history and thus to insure human survival, Faulkner subtly alters the reader's position. No longer are we active participants in the process of articulating truths about human experience. Instead of promoting an exchange between teller and reader, these novels make the reader the receptor of declared truths. The reader's role is clearly more passive than that which *The Sound and the Fury* or *Absalom* cultivates, although Faulkner does intend his words to persuade and to influence behavior. The most significant aspect of this change is the implicit declaration that meaning, or truth, does indeed reside in the words rather than in the exchange between the writer's words and the reader's comprehension of them. Much of the language in these novels has more in common with Bakhtin's definition of authoritative discourse than with the internally persuasive language of the everyday world and of the novel. At least, it aspires to the transcendence characteristic of such discourse: "The authoritative word is located in a distanced zone, organically connected with a past that is felt to be hierarchically higher. It is, so to speak, the word of the fathers" (Bakhtin, "Discourse in the Novel," 342). Bakhtin continues to say that the authoritative word, because it is inert and closed off from other words that would alter it, has never been successful in the novel, whose very concept is multivoiced. The point helps to explain the problems with *Requiem* and *A Fable*, both of which try in many and various words to assert enough power over the reader to change behavior. A brief look at one stylistic habit, a varied use of the negative, that punctuates all of Faulkner's writing illustrates the issue of power at work in all the novels, most particularly in the later ones.

Faulkner's language works to persuade us of the efficacy of language in the face of its limitations and the world's potential emptiness. The negative is the perfect vehicle for that purpose.[20] Any negative appears before us as a denial, as an apparent limitation, but Faulkner understood that implicit in the negative is the assertion of possibility. In addition, the abundance of negatives in his work stands as a tribute to the power of language. In *Language as Symbolic Action*, Kenneth Burke asserts that "the essential distinction between the verbal and the nonverbal is the fact that language adds the peculiar possibility of the Negative."[21] Burke's theory extends Henri Bergson's assertion in *Creative Evolution* that negative conditions cannot exist in nature. Burke reasons that the negative is then purely linguistic. He gets to the heart of the idea with which Faulkner wrestled all his life when he says that because all language requires the recognition that the word is not the thing, the "negative is of the very essence of language" (Burke, *Language as Symbolic Action*, 457). Thus the presence of the negative asserts an affirmation of language. But the most powerful aspect of the Faulknerian negative is its capacity to embody possibility and limitation at the same time.

Implicit in Faulkner's attempt to persuade us of the efficacy of language is the belief that language is both concept and precept. In other words, language not only articulates, and thus makes accessible all concepts, but it constitutes action as well.

Burke connects this dual function to the negative and locates its perfection in the Bible: "The negative must have begun as a rhetorical or hortatory function, *as with the negatives of the Ten Commandments*" (*Language as Symbolic Action*, 421, italics his). Faulkner, as well, saw the negative as an arbiter of behavior, but his vision is somewhat more complicated, as a brief return to *Intruder in the Dust* illustrates. Here Gavin Stevens tries to help his nephew understand why the town mob ran from Lucas Beauchamp, the man they had wronged:

> They simply repudiated not even in horror but in absolute unanimity a shall-not and should-not which without any warning whatever turned into a *must*-not. *Thou shalt not kill* you see—no accusative, heatless: a simple moral precept; we have accepted it in the distant anonymity of our forefathers . . . *we shall not kill* and maybe next time we even wont . . . *Thou shalt not kill* in precept and even when you do, precept still remains unblemished and scarless; . . . But *Gowrie must not kill Gowrie's brother*: no maybe about it, no next time to maybe not Gowrie kill Gowrie because there must be no first time. (199–200)

Gavin's explanation hinges on the proferring of the Sixth Commandment as "a simple moral precept." Like Burke, he directly connects a person's behavior to its governance by the most fundamental series of negatives in the Judeo-Christian heritage. In doing so, he affirms the power of language and the negative as the fundamental embodiment of that power. Negatives imply action, not nothing. But Gavin's experience with frail humanity leads him to recognize the limitations of language as precept. As an addendum to the command, "maybe next time we even wont" acknowledges humanity's willful disregard of it. Words can guide, but not guarantee; we are the variable. When Gavin adds that the precept remains "unblemished and scarless," he pays tribute to its intransigence among a people who continually exploit the difference between "shall-not" and "must-not." The commandment does demand a particular standard of action, but Gavin knows that although the taboo against fratricide still holds, people will interpret and even ignore some words at their own will. He articulates the uneasy recognition that any author must relinquish ownership of words once they are in print.

The negative also contains its antithesis. Burke comments that the Sixth Commandment "also has about its edges the positive *image* of killing" (*Language as Symbolic Action*, 10). In the same way, the words "unblemished and scarless" can convey the idea of smoothness as well as remind us of scars, something that "intact" or "perfect" cannot do. The ability to contain possibility while apparently ascribing limitations makes the negative eminently suitable for Faulkner's purpose. Through it he can demonstrate the plenitude of language by stretching its limitations. If words can be vague and deceptive, then Faulkner will dazzle us with abstractions. If habituated patterns and overuse have dulled some words into meaninglessness, Faulkner will force us to think hard about *his* words. As open to possibility as the negative can be, its biblical origins make it absolute. The Ten Commandments may contain the possibility of action or inaction, but they do not permit response. They remain intact from human alteration or answer and allow only obedience or disobedience. In its separation from context, the Word retains absolute authority.

And it is the single-voiced urgency, the aspiration to authority that defines *Requiem* and *A Fable*. In both, we are presented with examples and discussions, but Faulkner asserts and maintains complete control over the language. The moral purpose in both works is never sublimated for plot or character. Like the Ten Commandments, the books aspire to the power that will alter thought and action. Faulkner's fear that he would not live "long enough to have two sentences" certainly contributes to the greater authority of his words. The long preface to act 3 in *Requiem* includes the story of Cecelia Farmer, who scratched her name into the glass of a jailhouse window on April 16, 1861. The narrator interprets the gesture as Cecelia's statement to the world: "*'Listen, stranger: this was myself: this was I'*" (225). In refutation of Judith Sutpen's prediction that time and the elements will erase a person's scratches, Cecelia's "fragile and workless scratching" not only survives the years but remains legible and a testament to her existence. The same faith that words will defy mortality informs all of *Requiem for a Nun*, as well as *A Fable*.

Throughout the two works, Faulkner reinforces the connection he makes between the past and saying it all. A key element in the process of telling everything is, for Faulkner, telling the history of humanity. And an essential part of Faulkner's genre-mixing is his blurring of the distinctions between history and fiction. In both novels, the fictional plot unfolds against the background of actual and imagined historical events. The effect is to remind us that history is as much its author's interpretation as fiction is and that fiction is as true as history. The desire to put particular, present-day events into historical perspective indicates more than Faulkner's belief in the interdependence of past, present, and future time. Both *Requiem* and *A Fable* contain a preponderance of historical narrative. The large number of pages devoted to history indicates a mind that sees human experience as *story* and that believes absolutely in the ordering and controlling powers of articulation.

A closer examination of the ways that Faulkner constructs the two novels reveals his view of history and fiction. *Requiem for a Nun* is a three-act play that includes long sections of narrative. Borrowing from two genres to tell his story, Faulkner makes something more than either. Alongside the drama of Temple Drake's confrontation with the sins of her past, Faulkner unfolds the history of Jefferson, Mississippi. The introductory section of act 2 begins with the birth of the courthouse in Jackson and swells to a general history of the South. Altogether the prose sections comprise nearly two-thirds of the entire book. The structure does create a "contrapuntal effect which comes in orchestration"; it also speaks to Faulkner's need to say everything.[22] The preface to act 3 is one, forty-three page sentence that draws together all the major elements in Yoknapatawpha history within the framework of Cecelia Farmer's name etched on the jailhouse window. Both the play and the prose sections illuminate Faulkner's belief that the past determines the present. The two parts complement each other by repeatedly asking us to see connections, causes, and results. They also remind us of Faulkner's continued experimentation with the idea of the word as dialogue.

While the prose sections in *Requiem* do augment Temple Drake's crisis of conscience, inherent in their very existence is the need not merely to say it all, but to say it all again and again. Faulkner retells parts of *Absalom, Sartoris,* and *The Unvanquished* in the prose sections; he also repeats ideas from the first section in the other two sections of *Requiem.* And in each narrative, he moves forward in time by first going back into the past. Within the play itself, we see the relation of past to present very quickly, for Temple must deal with a guilt that started when Popeye raped her eight years before, thus continuing *Sanctuary.* Again Gavin is there to articulate more concisely the explanation: " 'The past is never dead. It's not even past.' " His pronouncement is definitive and echoes the Bible's absoluteness. Although the repetition is reinforcing rather than redundant, the fact that it exists at all indicates the strength of Faulkner's belief that turning experience into recapitulative narrative will make his readers remember it.

Faulkner also designs *A Fable* by employing several means to tell his story. The title names the genre from which he takes one method—the novel does relate, in fablelike fashion, a series of exploits during World War I, and it certainly makes an edifying, even cautionary point. Faulkner also draws on the story of Christ's life and death in an allegory that has caused almost as much confusion as the episode of the three-legged horse. Both the Christian allegory and the tall tale strain the limits of credibility, but they are entirely in keeping with Faulkner's interest in combining varied discourse to include all aspects and consider all the ramifications of his subject. And again, as in *Requiem,* he unfolds his subject by detailing its origins and evolution. Several times in the novel, the narrator digresses with lengthy history lessons. Writing to Malcolm Cowley, Faulkner describes his efforts in *A Fable* as "still trying to put all mankind's history in one sentence."[23] By centering his story on the Christian myth, Faulkner establishes a wide historical and moral framework.

Throughout *A Fable*, Faulkner casts present action into narrative or defines it by a surrounding historical context to grant it immediate and special significance. The Christian allegory lends specific meaning to the story of the corporal and the twelve men in his squad who organize the mutiny to stop the war. In retelling the story of Christ's life through the corporal, Faulkner makes sacred text secular. The process, common to Western thought since the Renaissance, gives a higher power to human imagination. As M. H. Abrams asserts in *Natural Supernaturalism*, the author assumes the role of revealing the way to salvation. Although Abrams' subject is the Romantic poets, his discussion of the characteristics of biblical history illuminates Faulkner's theory of history.[24] *A Fable* literally retells the life of Christ—"the same thing all them two thousand years ago"[25]—in the hope that this time we will listen. Also implicit in the novel's design is Faulkner's own assumption of the tenets of biblical history. He views our sojourn on earth as punctuated by apocalyptic events; and although he is always mindful of our capacity for self-destruction, Faulkner believes strongly that the best is yet to be. Like the Romantics before him, Faulkner shifts the burden of humanity's destruction and salvation from God to us. And he clearly places great faith in the redemptive powers of the imagination. The corporal cannot stop a people so bent on destroying themselves, but Faulkner's novel can if people will only listen to his voice. Faulkner commits the ultimate act of power by making the Christ figure a corporal, by incorporating sacred myths into secular history, and by telling the story through modern sensibilities, using the rhythms and design of the Bible. In these ways, his words become the Word.

The narrator of *A Fable* continually strengthens the connections between history and the power of words by placing events against the eternal, venerable backdrop of the past's grandest or most apocalyptic moments. Not since *Go Down, Moses* has Faulkner so concentrated his efforts to write his way to the place where all can be said. Again his method is to go back into the past. The English runner listens to Sutterfield's story of the groom and his three-legged horse, a parable of endurance and love. Then like Quentin and Ike, he is drawn into the immediacy of the past: "Five years afterward [he] was seeing what the Federal deputy marshall had [seen] five years ago while in the middle of it" (*Fable*, 129). At one point the narrator interrupts his description of the old general watching a flag-folding ceremony with a four-page delineation of the hierarchy of power in all wars. In the horse thief episode, a Mississippi lawyer is compared ironically to "the giants who co-erced compelled directed and, on occasion, actually led his myriad moil: Caesar and Christ, Bonaparte and Peter and Mazarin and Alexander" (153). One of the most extravagant illustrations of the tendency to aggrandize events through language occurs in the narrator's description of "the crippled horse and the English groom" as

> the immortal pageant-piece of the tender legend beginning when his first paired children lost well the world and from which paired prototypes they still challenged paradise, still paired and still immortal against the chronicle's grimed and blood-stained pages: Adam and Lilith and Paris and Helen and Pyramus and Thisbe . . . the world's oldest and most shining tale limning in his brief turn the warped-legged foul-mouthed English horse-groom as ever Paris or Lochinvar . . . the doomed glorious frenzy of a love-story. (*Fable*, 129)

The hyperbole and incongruity in the passage do indicate that the narrator sees the irony in the association he makes. But his continued reference to the groom's absolute devotion to his impossible horse finally undermines the humor. The passage is typical of the Faulknerian style that swells sentences to paragraphs as a single thought accumulates detail after detail. Here the narrator reinforces his point with every new phase and clause. By naming the immortal lovers, repeating key words, and continually restating the fact that present circumstances fit the "tender legend," the narrator encases the groom and the horse in language. In an

extravagant verbal exhibition, the narrator creates his own addition to the "immortal pageant piece." Faulkner enacts the desire
to preserve an idea in language that plagues all five of his men of
words.

The fact that Faulkner acts repeatedly on the impulse toward
inclusiveness reveals the strength and urgency in his commitment
to the word. This too is reflected in the biblical tone and design
that informs both novels. In delineating his "theory of genres,"
Northrop Frye names the Bible as our "central encyclopaedic
form." His words about the inclusive design of the Bible tells us
much about Faulkner's own approach to his novels: "For most
readers, myth, legend, historical reminiscence and actual history
are inseparable in the Bible, and even what is historical fact is not
there because it is 'true' but because it is mythically significant."[26]
Faulkner takes from myth and legend and history, from the sacred
and the secular, and writes his own version of human history.
Bakhtin would say that Faulkner's struggle with the words of
another, of an authority, is all part of the process of creating
internally persuasive discourse. But in *A Fable* and *Requiem*
particularly, the struggle against authority becomes redirected
toward Faulkner's own authority. All parts of the history he tells
increase the significance of the mythic truths about life that Faulkner always gives precedence to over facts.

The prelude to act 2 of *Requiem* exhibits precisely Faulkner's
movement toward absolute authority. The section, a history of the
Jackson courthouse as the embodiment of justice, is titled "The
Golden Dome (Beginning Was the Word)" (87). By reshaping Sacred Writ, "In the beginning was the Word, and the Word was
with God, and the Word was God" (John 1:1), Faulkner asserts his
own power. His words become the authoritative discourse; they
are he, the point of origin. From that imposing introduction, Faulkner proceeds with a brief catalog of Jackson's topography and
then, still in the same sentence, describes the birth of the courthouse. The effect is to make the courthouse a mythic structure
steeped in history and thus more significant. His language pushes
the courthouse far back into history: "In the beginning was already
decreed this rounded knob." The biblical allusions immediately

summon for the narrator the ultimate power. His words, he tells us, are original—they establish him as the creator of the golden dome. The language of the Christian text allows Faulkner to write a secular creation myth. In doing so, he establishes himself, the author, as its god.

Alongside the biblical phrasing are locutions that suggest a primeval world: "the earth tilted further to recede the sea rim by necklace-rim of crustacean husks" (*Requiem*, 88). From there, Faulkner writes his way back into the present day, which he covers with a chamber-of-commerce-like list of Jackson's particular features. The history and the sentence cover eleven pages. The tone is at times nostalgic, "those days were gone, the old brave innocent tumultuous eupeptic tomorrowless days" (91), lingering over the past to memorialize it and to relive it through language.

The narrator of this history declares the golden dome's inevitable and absolute presence, and in doing so, he also declares the absolute power of his words to provide full, immediate, and enduring context for his subject:

> In 1903 the new Capitol was completed—the golden dome, the knob, the gleamy crumb, the gilded pustule longer than the miasma and the gigantic ephemeral saurians, more durable than the ice and the pre-night cold, soaring, hanging as one blinding spheroid above the center of the Commonwealth, incapable of being either looked full or evaded, peremptory, irrefragible, and reassuring. (96–97)

The force of this passage comes not from a swift or climactic narrative action. The pace is languorous at best—the only new information we receive comes in the first and most direct clause. The reiteration of the same idea in the same words he has used throughout acts as a mnemonic device for the reader; the narrator clearly wants his words to have a lasting impression. This small section is also a summary of the history we have already read. The narrator moves from 1903 to prehistoric reptiles and the Ice Age to the present, thus condensing and mimicking the movement of the entire prelude. Made venerable by its timelessness, the dome also manifests the qualities of an absolute authority. The passage closes with a list of adjectives that attempt to name every element in our contradictory relation to authority. The words suggest a number of attitudes, and an apparent neologism suggests two at once. The word *irrefragible* is a combination of *irrefragable*, meaning "indisputable," and *irrefrangible*, which means "indestructible." Faulkner borrows from both to double the significance of the dome in a single new word. While acknowledging the dialogic nature of language in the very revision, the meaning of the word and the act of making it establish Faulkner's power.

The paragraph in *Requiem* is representative of two distinct stylistic habits that are characteristic of the entire narrative. And the tendencies toward inclusiveness and repetition also appear prominently in *A Fable*. The language continuously seeks to reveal everything at once while it also repeats the same idea, often verbatim. The notion that language can reveal all grants the word an enormous power. Lengthy, inclusive sentences are the most obvious evidence of Faulkner's faith in the power of language to tell all. Biblical allusions and elaborate diction also assert his verbal control. Against the backdrop of eternal truths and with the sheer force of vocabulary, Faulkner makes his case. Yet he betrays a certain anxiety about the extent of his power each time he duplicates a previously mentioned idea or phrase. Repetition is a primary rhetorical device in both novels, as if Faulkner must return to the beginning and restate his idea each time he wants to articulate it. Indeed the fact that he does return so frequently to the same ideas indicates their importance and also reveals some doubt about his power to articulate them sufficiently.

All remnants of the fears about the limitations in language that Faulkner argues explicitly and thoroughly in his earlier novels have been funneled into his prose style. No longer do characters or unidentified narrators doubt and test the efficiency of language; now Faulkner only acknowledges the persistence of those doubts in language that continues to argue against them. The only recourse he has against the limitations of language is his own power to state and restate. The effects of these doubts, particularly in *A Fable*, are an often rambling and confusing plot and an excess of language that threatens at times to overwhelm the reader. Sentences swollen with clause after clause fill the book. Most are too long to reproduce here, but the following description of the hall in which the war's leaders meet to discuss strategy illustrates Faulkner's tendency to overwrite:

> it still bore the imprint of that princely insensate (and perhaps one of the duchesses or marquises had thought, impregnable) opulence in its valenced alcoves and pilastered medallioned ceiling and crystal chandeliers and sconces and mirrors and girandoles and buhl étagères and glazed cabinets of faience bibelots, and a white rug into which war-bleached boots sank ankle-deep as into the muck of trenches, say in the cold face of the moon, flooring bland and soft as cloud, that majestic vista at the end of which the three old generals sat. (*Fable*, 192)

And this is only the last half of the sentence. Although the elaborate language mirrors the room's decor, its excesses also evince a compulsiveness about saying everything. At times, Faulkner says too much.

Repetition is, of course, not simply an indication of Faulkner's anxiety; saying it again also establishes the idea more firmly in the reader's mind. Saying it again keeps the idea alive. And Faulkner's primary concern in both *Requiem for a Nun* and *A Fable* is to articulate nothing less than the state of the world and to convince us of our responsibility to improve the conditions that our own prejudice and greed have created. If, as the old general in *A Fable* says, that "it will be [man's] own frankenstein which roasts him alive with heat, asphyxiates him with speech, wrenches loose his still-living entrails in the ferocity of its prey-seeking stoop" (299), then men *must* be made to listen. The most significant effect of this new urgency is to inject a good measure of Aristotelian rhetoric into the fiction. Faulkner knows well the persuasive nature of language and takes advantage of it now with greater intensity. Both *Requiem* and *A Fable* concern ideas. Although all of Faulkner's novels consider human experience, none concentrate so completely as these upon explicating general truths about the human condition.

In *Requiem for a Nun*, dialogues with Gavin Stevens and Nancy Mannigoe lead Temple Drake to a despairing recognition of responsibility for her past and her present. Gavin Stevens, "the bucolic Cincinnatus" (43), is Temple's lawyer, confidant, and finally the conarrator of Temple's tortured confession to the governor. As Ike does to Sam Fathers, Temple calls Gavin her "mouthpiece," and several times he interrupts the narrative that is clearly her means of comprehending her role in the tragedy. Unlike Sam's, Gavin's authority remains unchallenged. His remarks supply context and background and moderate Temple's self-punishing with motives and thus understanding. They also mimic the action of the narrator of the prose sections by insisting that Temple's past holds the key to her present. Finally, Gavin takes over the narrative: "I'm going to talk a while now" (138). And he does so at length, providing reasons for Temple's involvement with a series of inadequate men who figure prominently in her trouble. To do so, Gavin returns to the events recorded in *Sanctuary*, explaining motivations that Faulkner only suggests in the novel that he published twenty years earlier. Gavin's method is to narrate and interpret Temple's past; his effort makes the blackmail, adultery, and murder that mar it representative of all human folly. He and Temple speak in terms of saving her soul. The narration of her story uncovers the fundamental and difficult issues of sin, guilt, forgiveness, and salvation in an ambiguous world that complicates simple faith in God.

Gavin explains God's way to Temple through exegesis. Faulkner recalls the ambiguous passage that confounds Quentin Compson's grandfather in *Absalom*, but now Gavin Stevens gives the definitive reading: "When He said 'Suffer little children to come unto Me' He meant exactly that: He meant suffer . . . that the little children shall come unto Him unanguished, unterrified, undefiled" (141). Gavin's interpretation is different from either that the elder Compson can imagine, and more merciful. Protection of innocence is, of course, a more central issue in *Requiem*, but Gavin's assurance also echoes Faulkner's own authority. Temple, however, continues to ask the unanswerable questions. She does understand intellectually that the judicial system must punish Nancy Mannigoe to protect her young son's right to an innocent childhood, but she still questions a procedure that does not punish her own guilt.

Nancy Mannigoe understands this better than Temple because

she does not attempt to reason what can only be taken on faith. When Temple and Gavin visit Nancy in jail, they ask her about God's ways and receive only evidence of her simple, unquestioned faith: " 'I dont know. But I believes' " (241). Again Faulkner relies on his own idea of the black voice, which seems to exist primarily to guide more complex white folks.[27] Listening to Nancy, Temple begins to come to terms with her own inability to believe in God so utterly. The truths that Temple uncovers are difficult and rest on the frightening premise that we are free to sin and suffer. But the truths exist independent of Temple. Her task, like the reader's, is to assimilate the revelation, not to formulate truth. At the play's end, Temple names the equivocal state of the world: " 'Anyone to save it. Anyone who wants it. If there is none, I'm sunk. We all are. Doomed. Damned' " (245). Her words are deceptively final, for in rejoining her husband, Temple assumes her portion of guilt and suffering and decides to resume her life. The story of Cecelia Farmer introduces the last act of *Requiem*, and both women's gestures toward life reveal Faulkner's answer to humanity's doomed state. Cecelia's words and those of Temple herself refuse to accept oblivion. Temple's acceptance of herself and of life is the complicated and harder-won action of the two, but she and Cecelia share the desire to endure.

Temple Drake is not the only person that Faulkner, through Gavin, Nancy, and the prose narrator, seeks to convince. He constructs a novel that unfolds the history of Yoknapatawpha County in terms of humanity's moral development. Every element in the play and in the narrative contributes to Faulkner's definition of our position in a world that we have both inherited and made. The historical narratives put Temple Drake's particular dilemma into a larger context, explicitly giving universal significance to a specific drama. Although Gavin and Nancy both talk to persuade Temple of certain truths, it is the prose narrator who most emphatically makes known a particular vision of the world. The words order and interpret past events, making them more potent in the present because of the more informed perspective. Ultimately, Faulkner's play-novel asserts the tenacity of human beings and the unequaled capacity of language to assert it. Like all good rhetoricians, the narrator orders the final section climactically, ending with the person, a typical reader, who finds Cecelia's name:

> You know again now that there is no time: no space: no distance: a fragile and workless scratching almost depth-less in a sheet of old barely transparent glass . . . there is the clear undistanced voice . . . across the vast instantaneous intervention, from the long long time age: *'Listen, stranger; this was myself; this was I.'* (*Requiem*, 225)

The world will survive because the human instinct is to tell its story, to write its name. In the presence of a reader, the words will always speak and erase the barriers of time and space. Again the words assert meaning and the reader simply receives it. Clearly Faulkner intends for his own words to remove the boundaries that separate past, present, and future and to assert his truth and thus his existence.

Faulkner returns to the notion that language will save humans in *A Fable* when the old general finally meets with his son the corporal in an effort to persuade him to give up the mutiny and save himself. The general does almost all of the talking; here his belief in humanity elaborates Faulkner's Nobel Address:

> "(man's) puny and inexhaustible voice still talking, still planning; and there too after the last ding dong of doom had rung and died there will still be one sound more: his voice, planning to build something higher and faster and louder. . . . yet it too in the end will fail to eradicate him from the earth . . . man and his folly—"
> "Will endure," the corporal said.
> "They will do more." the old general said proudly. "They will prevail." (299–300)

The general's declaration ends his passionate, ten-page appeal to the corporal to relinquish his commitment to pacifism and thus spare him the anguish of ordering his son's death. The general does not convince his son, who represents an ideal too removed from the mundane earth to survive. But the general's words do make a convincing, paradoxical, and even sympathetic case—to insure the survival of civilization, the war must continue. Significantly, the general talks about *he* and *they;* the third-person pronouns effectively remove him from human folly to allow his commentary upon it. No longer do we have characters like Quentin Compson who worry about sacrificing their personal identity for the sake of the narrative or Darl Bundren whose insanity is marked by his complete detachment from himself. The general's detachment is necessary, even preferable.

The meeting at the old Roman citadel above Paris provides Faulkner with the opportunity to deliver his own assessment of humanity. Although Faulkner does give the old general some of his own words, it would be wrong to assume that he is Faulkner's spokesman. The general understands and controls more of the world than his son, but Faulkner knows and controls much more. Faulkner has the entire novel, his creation, under his power—his position is distanced from the human folly about which he writes, although he is clearly persuasive and openly subjective. He places the two men above the city, yet within an historical context, and presents a world view that brings all of his assumptions about language into focus.

The meeting essentially provides a framework that allows for the articulation of key ideas. The words of this scene, like much of the novel, declare the state of the world. The general himself says " 'We are two articulations, self-elected . . . anyway postulated, not so much to defend as to test two inimical conditions . . . and—one of them—must perish' " (*Fable*, 294). The scene is set for debate, but evolves into something more: "They are not inimical really, there is no contest actually, they can even exist side by side" (294). The general's modification of the opposition between his idea of the world and his son's admits a complexity, if not a genuine dialogue, that Faulkner cultivates throughout a complicated novel. Although Faulkner does align himself more fully with the general's viewpoint, he also stands above the tragic moral dilemma of the father-warlord to tell the comprehensive story. The corporal's stand for peace must fail, but we must listen to his voice because he is the articulation of an ideal, an aspiration that we need. The task of Faulkner's language, then, is to explain humanity in terms of the universal compulsions and hopes that built civilization and now threaten to destroy it. Thus his language necessarily must encompass all contradiction. The word can articulate and order a long and confusing history, but more important, it does so to stop our "enslavement to the demonic progeny of its own mechanical curiosity" (298). The ponderous, Latinate vocabulary underlines the seriousness of the subject.

Faulkner appears to place more faith in our capacity to prevail over our own "deathless folly" (298) than in our capacity to listen to the warning voice, but he does make a clear and strong assertion of his own power to change that. Because his task is so similar to the author's, the narrator illuminates Faulkner's own beliefs about the significance of creating narrative. *A Fable* opens with the unidentified narrator's description of the mass of citizens awaiting the arrival of the corporal and his twelve followers: "They had huddled all night in one vast tongueless brotherhood of dread and anxiety" (3). The words immediately establish the narrator as mouthpiece for the inarticulate masses. And he reiterates at every opportunity his vital function as the articulator for the "dense seething voiceless lake" (51) of humanity. Continually the narrator stresses the mob's inability to articulate itself, calling its sounds animal howling that pass "from gland to tongue without transition through thought" (187). The narrator's superiority derives from his capacity to articulate. He maintains the distance that he needs to view the masses, in part, through his condescension. Although the narrator seems to take unfair advantage to assert his power, he also mirrors the position that Faulkner himself takes in writing *A Fable.* Faulkner's compassion prevents outright condescension, but he does assume a position superior to the masses. The writer's responsibility is to chronicle human history, to detach himself from the living he sees around him in order to put all of it into words. Just as the old general and the corporal meet above the city to discuss the future of civilization, the narrator and the author must move away from the subject to see it clearly. In *A Fable,* Faulkner reasserts the concept of author-as-god that he makes explicit in *Requiem.*

Through the narrator, Faulkner establishes the conviction that language has the power to articulate and order human experience and thus to influence human behavior. *A Fable* tells us in countless ways that the very fate of the world rests on our capacity to stop our business and to listen to the voice that can predict our future by knowing our past and present. But Faulkner is not writing a political manifesto nor a history book, although at times he appears to do both. *A Fable* is part of the "bloodless lumberroom of literature" (212), as both the narrator and the quartermaster general refer to novels—the dusty depository for events, people, and ideas now gone from life. The description is less a comment upon literature than upon one very limiting attitude toward literature that *A Fable* seeks to improve. For it is the very nature of fiction that allows Faulkner to be historian, psychologist, tale-spinner, sage, and seer. The novelist can go beyond fact to tell the truth. And Faulkner takes full advantage of the special powers to create and to interpret that fiction allows him. *A Fable* is Faulkner's version of an actual war. To the fact of World War I, he supplies a complex of characters who represent all aspects of human behavior and who together explain the human origins and inevitable reasons for war. Individual motives become paradigms for shared human traits—both admirable and base. Specific actions always develop against the backdrop of human history. Unfortunately, Faulkner's efforts toward absolute authority do put *A Fable* in the "bloodless lumberroom."

The ideas about the state of humanity and the world that Faulkner elaborates are provocative and often quite moving. But in articulating those ideas, Faulkner also writes a difficult, ponderous novel filled with an outpouring of language that threatens, at times, to obscure his point. *A Fable* suffers more than *Requiem* from being a novel of ideas because Faulkner has charged himself with a world-scale moral responsibility. His words resound with the intensity of his convictions. The real significance of *A Fable* and *Requiem* lies not in their relative literary or ideological merits but in the conclusions about language that Faulkner reaches though them.

Images of the dying but persistent voice color both novels. In *Requiem*, the "clear undistanced voice" of the long-dead Cecelia Farmer speaks across the years; the narrator writes the Yoknapatawpha history because "even the simple dispossession of Indians begot in time a minuscule of archive, let alone the normal litter of man's ramshackle confederation against environment" (3); and as Temple Drake leaves the jail, the doomed Nancy Mannigoe calls out to her twice, " 'believe' " (243), in a last attempt to convince her. In *A Fable*, the old general talks of humanity's instinct for survival in terms of the " 'inexhaustible voice' " (299); the dying runner wheezes through his shattered teeth, " 'I'm not going to die' " (370); and the priest who kills himself because his faith is weak makes "a thin sweet crying of frustration and despair until the pinch of his hand between the bayonet's cross guard and his own flesh told him better and so he could stop the crying now—the sweet thick warm murmur of it pouring suddenly from his mouth" (313). Even in dying, the body communicates. Finally the narrators of both novels talk and talk against oblivion. Life is story, they tell us; the individual's word must compete against formidable odds to be heard, much less to influence. The words of the later novels do not forget the multivoiced world; rather, they urgently fight against it. The narratives present and explain humanity for the sake of preserving it, but behind every word is also William Faulkner's conviction that even after he dies, his words will remain to assert "not *might* have been, nor even *could* have been, but *was*" (*Requiem*, 225). And because Faulkner also asserts the indelible link between *was* and *is*, he forges his own immortality in language.

Notes   Works Cited   Index

Notes

1. Horace Benbow and Faulkner's Troubled Authority

1. William Faulkner, *Saratoris* (1929; reprint, New York: New American Library, Signet Classics, 1964), 282. Subsequent references to this edition will appear parenthetically in the text.

2. Jean Stein, "William Faulkner," *Paris Review*, 4 (Spring 1956), as reprinted in *Writers at Work: The Paris Review Interviews*, ed. Malcolm Cowley (New York: Viking Press, 1958), 123.

3. Frederick Gywnn and Joseph Blotner, eds., *Faulkner in the University* (Charlottesville: University Press of Virginia, 1977), 202.

4. Joseph Blotner, *Faulkner: A Biography*, 2 vols. (New York: Random House, 1974), 1:546. Subsequent references to this edition will appear parenthetically in the text.

5. In *The Crossing of the Ways* (New Brunswick, N.J.: Rutgers University Press, 1989), Karl F. Zender makes the point that this connection between Faulkner and Quentin suggests a way for Faulkner to affirm his own power "to encompass and order the manifold sounds of the world around him" (18). Quentin's anxieties, as Zender notes, are also Faulkner's. Zender's concerns are specifically with sound as a powerful agent in the fiction; mine are with the language that articulates it.

6. For a much fuller discussion of the Quentin-Ike connection see John W. Hunt, "The Disappearance of Quentin Compson," in *Critical Essays on William Faulkner: The Compson Family*, ed. Arthur F. Kinney (Boston: G. K. Hall, 1982), 366–80. Also Blotner explores the connections in *Faulkner* 1:1076–95.

7. The best discussion of the Horace-Gavin connection is Michael Millgate's "Faulkner's First Trilogy," in *Fifty Years of Yoknapatawpha*, ed. Doreen Fowler and Ann J. Abadie (Jackson: University Press of Mississippi, 1980), 90–109. Millgate's argument is most convincing in his discussion of textual connections between *Sanctuary* and *Re-*

quiem for a Nun that give Horace's thoughts about Popeye, for example, to Gavin.

8. See Joseph Blotner, "William Faulkner's Essay on the Composition of *Sartoris*," in *Yale University Library Gazette*, 47 (Jan. 1973): 122. Subsequent references will appear parenthetically in the text.

9. John T. Matthews, *The Play of Faulkner's Language* (Ithaca, N.Y.: Cornell University Press, 1982). For a full account of Derrida's principle of *difference* and how it helps to explain the constant sense of deferment in Faulkner's fiction, see 26–27.

10. Walter J. Slatoff, *Quest for Failure: A Study of William Faulkner* (Ithaca, N.Y.: Cornell University Press, 1960). Others who have added to the discussion of language as barrier or revealer of truth are Arthur Kinney, *Faulkner's Narrative Poetics: Style as Vision* (Amherst: University of Massachusetts Press, 1978); Eric Larsen, "The Barrier of Language: The Irony of Language in Faulkner," *Modern Fiction Studies* 12 (Spring 1967): 19–31; and Karl Zink, "Flux and the Frozen Moment: The Imagery of Stasis in Faulkner's Prose," *PMLA* 71 (June 1956): 285–301.

11. John Irwin, *Doubling and Incest/Repetition and Revenge* (Baltimore: Johns Hopkins University Press, 1980), 63, 69, 114.

12. Irwin, *Doubling and Incest*, 158. Irwin also presents a provocative discussion of Faulkner's recognition that writing entails the death of a part of the author's self.

13. In "Answering as Authoring: Mikhail Bakhtin's Trans-Linguistics," Michael Holquist gives an extensive discussion of Bakhtin's "vision of language as constant struggle," an idea very close to Faulkner's. In *Bakhtin: Essays and Dialogues on His Work*, ed. Gary Saul Morson (Chicago: University of Chicago Press, 1986), 59–71.

14. Mikhail Bakhtin, "Discourse in the Novel," in *The Dialogic Imagination: Four Essays*, ed. Michael Holquist; trans. Caryl Emerson and Michael Holquist (Austin: University of Texas Press, 1981), 266. Subsequent references to this edition will appear parenthetically in the text.

15. Gywnn and Blotner, eds., *Faulkner in the University*, 45.

16. Wayne C. Booth, "Freedom of Interpretation: Bakhtin and the Challenge of Feminist Criticism," in *Bakhtin: Essays and Dialogues on His Work*, ed. Gary Saul Morson (Chicago: University of Chicago Press, 1986), 145–76.

17. At the matrix of all such criticism are Myra Jehlen's book *Class and Character in Faulkner's South* (New York: Columbia University Press, 1976) and André Bleikasten's essay "For/Against an Ideological Reading of Faulkner's Novels," in *Faulkner and Idealism: Perspectives from Paris*, ed. Michael Gresset and Patrick Samway, S.J. (Jackson: University Press of Mississippi, 1983), 27–50. Although not di-

rectly concerned with Faulkner's language, Eric Sundquist's study of Faulkner and racial history is invaluable in tracing the connections between the language and the issue that produced some of his best work. See *Faulkner: The House Divided* (Baltimore: Johns Hopkins University Press, 1983). Also I find Darwin T. Turner's essay "Faulkner and Slavery" particularly helpful in delineating the roots of Faulkner's perspective. In *The South and Faulkner's Yoknapatawpha*, ed. Evans Harrington and Ann J. Abadie (Jackson: University Press of Mississippi, 1977), 62–85. Faulkner's women get perhaps their fullest treatment in Sally R. Page's book *Faulkner's Women: Characterization and Meaning* (Deland, Fla.: Everett/ Edwards, 1972). Page's readings are strictly inside patriarchal notions of the female, but she does sensitively articulate the ideology out of which Faulkner himself wrote. Two more rigorously contentious, and therefore illuminating, studies of Faulkner's women in general are Sergei Chakovsky's "Women in Faulkner's Novels: Author's Attitude and Artistic Function" and Myriam Diaz-Diocartez's "Faulkner's Hen-House: Woman as Bounded Text." Both in *Faulkner and Women*, ed. Doreen Fowler and Ann J. Abadie (Jackson: University Press of Mississippi, 1985), 41–57, 235–69.

18. Blotner notes that Faulkner was too distraught over the rejection of *Flags* to do much of the actual cutting. Ben Wasson, who had served as Faulkner's model for Horace, reduced or deleted much of the narrative about Horace's sexual involvement and his sense of doom. See *Faulkner* 1:546 and 580–84. Also see Gerald Langford, *Faulkner's Revision of "Sanctuary"* (Austin: University of Texas Press, 1972), 3–33, for a thorough discussion of the original manuscript. Noel Polk, editor of *Sanctuary: The Original Text* (New York: Random House, 1981), discusses Faulkner's particular attachment to Horace, 293–306.

19. See Noel Polk, "The Space Between *Sanctuary*," in *Intertextuality in Faulkner*, ed. Michel Gresset and Noel Polk (Jackson: University Press of Mississippi, 1985), 36–56. An earlier version of this essay was entitled " 'The Dungeon Was Mother Herself': William Faulkner: 1927–1931" and appeared in *New Directions in Faulkner Studies*, ed. Doreen Fowler and Ann J. Abadie (Jackson: University Press of Mississippi, 1984), 61–93.

20. See James G. Watson, *William Faulkner: Letters and Fictions* (Austin: University of Texas Press, 1987), 66–67. By observing the conjunctions between Faulkner's letters and his fiction, Watson reinforces the idea that Faulkner's anxieties about language, sex, and death are at least partially manifest in Horace Benbow. (Note that subsequent references to this edition will appear parenthetically in the text.)

21. William Faulkner, *Flags in the Dust* (New York: Random House, Vintage Books, 1973), 170. Subsequent references to this edition will appear parenthetically in the text.

22. William Faulkner, *Sanctuary* (1931; corrected text, New York: Random House, Vintage Books, 1987), 27. Subsequent references to this edition will appear parenthetically in the text.

23. William Faulkner, "Une Ballad des Femmes Perdues," *William Faulkner: Early Prose and Poetry*, ed. Carrel Collins (Boston: Little, Brown and Co., 1962), 54.

24. Faulkner's own affinity for poetry, particularly for Keats, strengthens his personal ties to Horace Benbow. Certainly Faulkner understood Horace's love of poetry very well. See James Meriwether and Michael Millgate, eds., *Lion in the Garden* (Lincoln: University of Nebraska Press, 1968), 134–35. The connection between Horace's idealism and Keats' "Ode on a Grecian Urn" is given brief but provocative mention in John Irwin's *Doubling and Incest*, 169. Olga Vickery also notes the connection and discusses it in light of Horace's fervent belief in rightness and order in *The Novels of William Faulkner* (Baton Rouge: Louisiana State University Press, 1964), 23 and 104–14. For further reading see Linda E. McDaniel, "Horace Benbow: Faulkner's Endymion," *Mississippi Quarterly* 33 (Summer 1980): 363–70 and Myles Hurd, "Faulkner's Horace: The Burden of Characterization and the Confusion of Meaning in *Sanctuary*," *College Language Association Journal* 23 (June 1980): 416–30. I find James Watson, *Letters and Fictions*, helpful in making concrete the connections between Faulkner and Horace. As he shows, it is their attraction to an idealized worded haven that is most similar.

25. Karl Zender notes that Faulkner's own poetry is often as remote from worldly contamination. He then argues that with the writing of *Flags*, Faulkner moves into a voiced world of his South. Zender's focus on sound as a disruptive force in the fiction offers a provocative perspective on the issue of authorial control. *Crossing*, 3–12. See also Watson, *Letters and Fictions*, 71–72.

26. See Faulkner, "An Introduction to *The Sound and the Fury*," in *Faulkner: New Perspectives*, ed. Richard H. Brodhead (Englewood Cliffs, N.J.: Prentice-Hall, 1983), 27. (Subsequent references to this edition will appear parenthetically in the text.) Gail L. Mortimer's essay, "The Smooth, Suave Shape of Desire: Paradox in Faulknerian Imagery of Women" is an excellent reading of the desire for the clean shape of female purity in *Flags* and *Sanctuary;* Mortimer follows the paradoxical images of female chastity and corruption through all the major fiction and connects them to Faulkner's own life. In *Women's Studies* 13 (1986): 149–61.

27. T. S. Eliot, "The Love Song of J. Alfred Prufrock," in *The

Collected Poems of T. S. Eliot, 1909–1962 (New York: Harcourt Brace & World, 1970), line 52. See also Michel Gresset's discussion of Faulkner's borrowings in "The 'Dying Fall' in *Sanctuary* and *Murphy*" in *Intertextuality in Faulkner*, 57–72. For further discussion on Faulkner's use of Prufrock, see Cleanth Brooks, *William Faulkner: The Yoknapatawpha Country* (New Haven, Conn.: Yale University Press, 1963), 105–7.

28. Watson observes that one "law of letters is that the letter is always about itself," *Letters and Fictions*, 8.

29. See Matthews, *Play of Faulkner's Language*, 54–56. Also Judith Bryant Wittenberg notes that Horace's definition of lying makes writing "doomed [and] estranging, [yet] psychically necessary." See Wittenberg's essay, 328, "Vision and Re-Vision: Bayard Sartoris," in *Critical Essays on William Faulkner: The Sartoris Family*, ed. Arthur Kinney (Boston: G. K. Hall, 1985), 323–31.

30. See Jehlen, *Class and Character*, 1–17 and 42–43. Jehlen makes the central point that Faulkner's interest in perception in these novels comes out of his own knowledge that the truth he wants to articulate is somehow beyond his reach. In "For/Against an Ideological Reading," Bleikasten discusses Faulkner's desire for "the universal" and the critical perception of Faulkner as universal in the context of its value in Western culture (43–45).

31. In "*Sanctuary:* Style as Vision," Arthur F. Kinney interprets Horace's characterization as extremely negative. I share Kinney's dislike but think Faulkner's real indictment lies in the society that produces situations such as the one Horace tries to save; however, Kinney provides provocative discussion of the parallels between Popeye and Horace. Another view of the same issue is George Toles' "The Space Between: A Study of Faulkner's *Sanctuary*." Both articles appear in *Twentieth Century Interpretations of Sanctuary*, ed. J. Douglas Canfield (Englewood Cliffs, N.J.: Prentice-Hall, 1982), 109–19 and 120–28.

32. Robert Parker discusses the central gap in the text at length in *William Faulkner and the Novelistic Imagination* (Champaign-Urbana: University of Illinois Press, 1985), 59–86, and he makes a convincing case for Faulkner's identification with Horace.

33. See Bleikasten, "Of Sailboats and Kites: The 'Dying Fall' in Faulkner's *Sanctuary* and Beckett's *Murphy*," in *Intertextuality in Faulkner*, ed. Michel Gresset and Noel Polk (Jackson: University Press of Mississippi, 1985), 35–56.

34. See Jehlen, *Class and Character*, 28–41, for a discussion of Faulkner's participation in and partial rejection of aristocratic culture in *Flags*.

35. See Turner, "Faulkner and Slavery," 65. For another discussion

of Caspey as betraying white anxiety over racism see Erskine Peters, *William Faulkner: The Yoknapatawpha World and Black Being* (Darby, Pa.: Norwood Editions, 1983), 42–43.

36. See Gerald Langford, *Faulkner's Revision of "Sanctuary": A Collation of Unrevised Galleys and the Published Book* (Austin: University of Texas Press, 1972), 3–5, for Faulkner's remarks about revising *Sanctuary* because "it might sell; maybe 10,000 of them will buy it" and a discussion of critical response.

37. The collection of essays published from the 1985 Yoknapatawpha Conference, "Faulkner and Women," provides a fairly comprehensive look at critical interpretations of Faulkner's women that move beyond scholars like Cleanth Brooks who praise Faulkner's tribute to female moral superiority and courage (*William Faulkner: The Yoknapatawpha Country* and his Introduction to Sally R. Page's book, *Faulkner's Women*, xi–xxii), and Leslie Fiedler who charges that Faulkner reduces women to a series of negative stereotypes (*Love and Death in the American Novel* [New York: Stein and Day, 1975]). Particularly helpful as an overview is Ilse Dusoir Lind's "The Mutual Relevance of Faulkner's Studies and Women's Studies: An Interdisciplinary Inquiry," in Doreen Fowler and Ann J. Abadie's *Faulkner and Women*, 21–40. This essay sets the stage for feminist interpretations of Temple Drake.

38. Robert Parker gives a sensible and straightforward defense of the position that Temple's youth and state of shock account for her behavior. He also notes Temple's later behavior as the creation of misogynist thinking, but he is much more willing than I to overlook all of the indications that Faulkner cannot get outside the definition of female that the novel upholds (*Novelistic Imagination*, 62–65). Others have resisted Temple Drake's metamorphosis from victim to victimizer, but most attribute—erroneously I think—Temple's innocence as Faulkner's intention. See Dianne Luce Cox, "A Measure of Innocence: *Sanctuary's* Temple Drake," *The Mississippi Quarterly*, 39 (Summer 1986): 301–24.

39. See Parker *Novelistic Imagination*, 1–4, for a full discussion of this point.

2. Quentin Compson: Isolation and the Power of Exchange

1. William Faulkner, *The Sound and the Fury* (1929; reprint, New York: Random House, Vintage Books, 1954), 219–20. Subsequent references to this edition will appear parenthetically in the text.

2. Gwynn and Blotner, eds., *Faulkner in the University*, 262–63.

3. Gwynn and Blotner, eds., *Faulkner in the University*, 95.

4. Olga Vickery makes this point in *Novels of William Faulkner*, 39.

5. William Faulkner, *Absalom, Absalom!* (1936; corrected text, New York: Random House, Vintage Books, 1987), 313. Subsequent references to this edition will appear parenthetically in the text.

6. Floyd C. Watkins discusses Faulkner's aversion to abstract language in *The Flesh and the Word: Eliot, Hemingway, Faulkner* (Nashville: Vanderbilt University Press, 1971), 169–276. Watkins says that Quentin lives by an abstract, meaningless code, which is true, but only a partial explanation of his problem.

7. Matthew Arnold, "The Function of Criticism," in *Poetry and Criticism of Matthew Arnold*, ed. A. Dwight Culler (Boston: Houghton Mifflin Co., Riverside, 1961), 256.

8. For another discussion of the "linguistic nature" of Quentin's sexual problems, see Stephen M. Ross, "The 'Loud World' of Quentin Compson," in *Studies in the Novel* 7 (Summer 1975): 254.

9. Irwin, *Doubling and Incest*, 114–15.

10. Ross, " 'Loud World,' " 252.

11. See Irwin for a thorough discussion of the narrative as a means for Quentin to explore the relationships among Caddy, Dalton Ames, and himself (*Doubling and Incest*, 50–52). Robert Parker gives a particularly convincing reading of Quentin's and Faulkner's horror of miscegenation (*Novelistic Imagination*, 138–46).

12. See John Matthews' argument for the act of narration as the novel's center rather than a search for the definitive story of Thomas Sutpen (*Play of Faulkner's Language*, 115–61). Matthews sees the collaboration between Shreve and Quentin as the embodiment of Faulkner's theory that language is always a process of deferment of absolute signifiers.

13. See Matthews, *Play of Faulkner's Language*, 82–83, for a discussion of Quentin's failure.

14. James Watson notes that neither we nor anyone in the novel knows the contents of Quentin's letters, a significant play for authority and closure. Watson also discusses all the written communications in *The Sound and the Fury*, particularly Jason's, in some detail. See *Letters and Fictions*, 76–91.

15. See Gwynn and Blotner, eds., *Faulkner in the University*, 1.

16. André Bleikasten's *The Most Splendid Failure* (Bloomington: Indiana University Press, 1976) contains a chapter on Caddy as the "deceptive echo of a name" throughout the novel; see 43–66 in particular. Also see John Irwin's discussion of Quentin's psychological motiva-

tions for telling the incest story (*Doubling and Incest*, 37–51) and John Matthews' discussion of the novel's repeated recognitions of loss (*Play of Faulkner's Language*, 63–114).

17. Bleikasten reads Benjy's "trying to say" as the mirror of the novel's many attempts to tell its story; and Matthews builds from there to assert Faulkner's belief that the failure to fix on an absolute meaning is responsible for the story's prolonged life. I would add that the novel also explores and successfully establishes communication between reader and narrative that is about the tragedy of being without words. See Bleikasten, *The Most Splendid Failure*, 83–84 and Matthews, *Play of Faulkner's Language*, 71–73.

18. John Matthews notes that Jason's word manifests itself in his conviction that he has silenced his family's problems by making life an economic issue, *Play of Faulkner's Language*, 92.

19. See Matthews, *Play of Faulkner's Language*, 91.

20. From Martin Grotjahn's analysis of Freud and wit in "Beyond Laughter," in *Theories of Comedy*, ed. Paul Lauter, Jr. (New York: Doubleday & Co., 1964), 524.

21. Both Bleikasten and Matthews give interpretations of Faulkner's method in section 4 that correctly direct our attention to Faulkner's deliberate avoidance of ultimate resolutions. Bleikasten discusses Faulkner's conjectural method as the failed attempt to restore the absolute presence of language to itself, *The Most Splendid Failure*, 176 and 204–6. Matthews points to Faulkner's own words on finishing the novel repeatedly with each section as the oxymoron that describes the novel's dilemma of refusing any word special authority, (*Play of Faulkner's Language*, 105). Their conclusions also underscore Faulkner's awareness that the power of language lies in its ability to *suggest*, that the dynamic between writer and reader is one of perpetual possibility. I would add that section 4 also reminds us, with even more authority than the others can, that because language is subjective, it does tell us about the consciousness behind the words we read.

22. The glorification of Dilsey's suffering is extended to the entire congregation and is a reminder that Faulkner's black people are definitely a white person's creation. For readings grounded in the belief that Faulkner wants to escape language, see Paul R. Lilly, "Caddy and Addie: Speakers of Faulkner's Impeccable Language," *Journal of Narrative Technique* 3 (Sept. 1973): 170–82 and Eric Larsen, "Barrier of Language," 21–22.

23. Among the most provocative work done on Faulkner's engagement with language and narration are David Krause, "Reading Bon's Letter and Faulkner's *Absalom, Absalom!*" *PMLA* 99 (1984): 225–41, Matthews' chapter in *Play of Faulkner's Language*, 116–61, and

Stephen Ross, "Oratory and the Dialogical in *Absalom, Absalom!*" in *Intertextuality in Faulkner*, 73–86.

24. Ross, "Oratory and the Dialogic," 79–80. Also see Nancy Blake, "Creation and Procreation: The Voice and the Name, or Biblical Intertextuality in *Absalom, Absalom!*" in *Intertextuality in Faulkner*, 128–43. Blake also comments on the single-voicedness of *Absalom*.

25. James Watson's discussion of the letters in *Absalom* underscores Faulkner's own intensely personal involvement in his manuscript. See *Letters and Fictions*, 114–29.

26. On the issue of the success of Faulkner's figurative language, I disagree with James Guetti who asserts that no metaphor is ever constructed in *Absalom*, thus preserving Faulkner's belief that potential meaning must always remain unrealized. See *The Limits of Metaphor* (Ithaca, N.Y.: Cornell University Press, 1967), 108.

27. In "Reading Bon's Letter," David Krause notes that Mr. Compson wants to read Bon's letter as a document, trying to find in it what he never knew. See 229–33 for a discussion of Compson as a historical reader.

28. The dialogue between Henry and Judith embodies the notion that "to say is to do" that J. L. Austin delineates in *How To Do Things With Words* (Cambridge: Harvard University Press, 1962), 6–8. Also see Ross for a discussion of this passage as dialogue that is "paradigmatic of all confrontations," in "Oratory and the Dialogical," 83.

29. Gywnn and Blotner, eds., *Faulkner in the University*, 84.

30. Stonum also cites *Pylon* (1935) as Faulkner's first novel to be written completely in the long, complex style. See *Faulkner's Career: An Internal Literary History* (Ithaca, N.Y.: Cornell University Press, 1979), 147.

31. Gywnn and Blotner, eds., *Faulkner in the University*, 273–74.

3. As I Lay Dying *and* Light in August: *Communities of Language*

1. See Blotner, *Faulkner*, 1:703.

2. The section of this chapter on *As I Lay Dying* is a revised version of an article first published in *Arizona Quarterly* (43 [Summer 1987]:165–77) titled "Language and the Process of Narration in Faulkner's *As I Lay Dying*." It is reprinted here with the permission of *Arizona Quarterly*.

3. Faulkner, *As I Lay Dying* (1930; corrected text, New York: Random House, Vintage, 1987), 157. Subsequent references to this edition will appear parenthetically in the text.

4. Because Addie's section is central to Faulkner's dialogue about the efficacy of language, I must acknowledge those critics whose work has enriched our perceptions of Addie and words. Although I disagree with Paul Lilly's argument that Addie speaks for Faulkner in endorsing the perfection of silence, his delineation of her desire to transcend language, epitomized by the blank space in her section, does locate one element of Faulkner's concern. See Lilly, "Caddy and Addie," 170–82. For further discussion of the problem that Addie's hatred of words also binds her to an absolute , deadening belief in them, see Panthea R. Broughton, *William Faulkner: The Abstract and the Actual* (Baton Rouge: Louisiana State University Press, 1974), 192; Constance Pierce, "Being, Knowing, and Saying in the 'Addie' Section of Faulkner's *As I Lay Dying*," *Twentieth Century Literature* 26 (1980): 294–305; and Olga Vickery, *Novels of William Faulkner*, 64. See as well André Bleikasten's discussion of language and power in *Faulkner's As I Lay Dying*, trans. Roger Little (Bloomington: Indiana University Press, 1973), 44–64 and 133–37.

5. William R. Allen addresses the Addie-Darl dialogue on language by aligning both with different but specifically poetic theories of language. In doing so, he dislocates Faulkner's concerns somewhat; John Matthews' assertion that Faulkner knows all efforts of the mind are structured by words is more to the point. William R. Allen, "The Imagist and Symbolist Views of the Function of Language: Addie and Darl Bundren in *As I Lay Dying*," *Studies in American Fiction* 10 (Autumn 1982): 185–96; Matthews, *Play of Faulkner's Language*, 15–62.

6. See also Ross' discussion of the distinction between character and narrator in the novel. Stephen Ross, " 'Voice' in Narrative Texts: The Example of *As I Lay Dying*," *PMLA* 94 (1979): 300–308.

7. For other readings of Darl's insanity, see William Rossky, "*As I Lay Dying*: The Insane World," *Texas Studies in Literature and Language* 4 (Spring 1962): 87–95, and Joseph M. Garrison, Jr., "Perception, Language, and Reality in *As I Lay Dying*," *Arizona Quarterly* 32 (1976): 16–30.

8. William Faulkner, *Mosquitoes* (1927; reprint, New York: Liveright, 1955), 251.

9. See Parker, *Novelistic Imagination*, 23–58. Parker mentions Cash-as-ennobled as one of several ways that readers try to make this strange text familiar and thus oversimplify it. His reading of the novel's resistance to our desire to describe it is a recognition of the other in language from a different perspective. Parker's word is *bothness* and with it he identifies the novel's determination "to be more than one thing at a time" (38). My reading focuses on how Faulkner's

awareness of duality informs his understanding of our language and his work.

10. William Faulkner, *Light in August* (1932; corrected text, New York: Random House, Vintage Books, 1987), 489, 495. Subsequent references to this edition will appear parenthetically in the text.

11. Eric Sundquist's reading of Faulkner and the issue of race in *Light in August* is particularly helpful because of Sundquist's careful examination of social history and the novel. His approach underscores the idea of heteroglossia in the novel. See Sundquist, *House Divided*, 63–95.

12. Myra Jehlen, *Class and Character*, 87–96.

13. André Bleikasten's essay on the novel as a closed system provides a superb delineation of that system, or community, as a reflection of white, male standards against which females and blacks necessarily must be viewed with suspicion. Noting their otherness in this novel, he argues convincingly that the other is turned into a figure of menace. See *"Light in August:* The Closed Society and Its Subjects" in *New Essays on Light in August*, ed. Michael Millgate (Cambridge: Cambridge University Press, 1987), 81–102.

14. Robert Parker's discussion of the misogyny in *Light in August* is one of the most sensible and provocative I have read. While I probably find the sexism more offensive than he, I do think Parker brings an important balance to the issue. See Parker, *Novelistic Imagination*, 102–7. Also, Judith Bryant Wittenberg's "The Women of *Light in August*" is a detailed and balanced study of the novel's misogyny. She skirts the issue of the narrator's voice which favors what the character's words reveal about attitudes, but otherwise she brings significant insights to the problem. See 103–22.

15. In "Joe Christmas and 'Womanshe negro,' " Doreen Fowler defends Faulkner against charges that he shares the racism and sexism in the novel. See her essay in *Faulkner and Women*, 144–61.

16. In *Faulkner's Women: The Myth and the Muse*, David Williams gives a careful delineation of Lena as the Earth Mother but does not take issue with the idea itself. See *Faulkner's Women* (Montreal: Queen's University Press, 1977), 157–84.

17. For more on the connections between characters and mythology, see Beach Langston, "The Meaning of Lena Grove and Gail Hightower in *Light in August*," *Boston University Studies in English* 5 (Spring 1961): 46–63; Robert M. Slabey, "Myth and Ritual in *Light in August*," *Texas Studies in Literature and Language* 2 (Autumn 1960): 328–49, and "Joe Christmas: Christ Figure, Villain, or Tragic Hero," series in *Twentieth Century Interpretations of Light in August*, ed. David L. Minter (Englewood Cliffs, N.J.: Prentice-Hall,

1969), 93–107, and André Bleikasten, "In Praise of Helen," in *Faulkner and Women*, 128–43.

18. The significance of the names in *Light in August* has generated a great deal of critical speculation. François Pitavy in *Faulkner's Light in August*, trans. Gillian E. Cook (Bloomington: Indiana University Press, 1973), 75–80, gives a good overview of the work. Also see Mario D'Avanzo "Bobbie Allen and the Ballad Tradition in *Light in August*," *South Carolina Review* 8 (Nov. 1975): 22–29.

19. See Vickery, *Novels of William Faulkner*, 281. My discussion of Faulkner's language is informed by those critics, beginning with Conrad Aiken, who have delineated and integrated the many elements of Faulkner's style. The two earliest articles on Faulkner's style are Conrad Aiken's "William Faulkner: The Novel as Form," 46–52, and Warren Beck's "William Faulkner's Style," 53–65, both in *Faulkner: A Collection of Critical Essays*, ed. Robert Penn Warren (Englewood Cliffs, N.J.: Prentice-Hall, 1966). More recently, Arthur F. Kinney's book, *Faulkner's Narrative Poetics*, makes a significant argument for Faulkner's belief in writing as a collaborative, ongoing process between writer and reader. For other discussions of general stylistic matters, see William Van O'Connor, "Rhetoric in Southern Writing: Faulkner," *Georgia Review* 12 (Spring 1958): 83–86; F. C. Riedel, "Faulkner as Stylist," *South Atlantic Quarterly* 56 (Autumn 1957): 462–79; and Albert J. Guerard, "Faulkner the Innovator," in *The Maker and the Myth*, ed. Evans Harrington and Ann Abadie (Jackson: University Press of Mississippi, 1978), 71–88.

4. Ike McCaslin and the Threatened Order

1. For an extended discussion of the effects of white paternalism as they are expressed in *Go Down, Moses* and in earlier works, see André Bleikasten's "Fathers in Faulkner," in *The Fictional Father: Lacanian Readings of the Text*, ed. Robert Con Davis (Amherst: University of Massachusetts Press, 1981), 115–46. Bleikasten connects the struggle to supersede the father, to establish one's own name with Faulkner's efforts in authoring.

2. William Faulkner, *Go Down, Moses* (1940; reprint, New York: Random House, Vintage Books, 1973), 191. Subsequent references to this edition will appear parenthetically in the text.

3. See Jehlen, *Class and Character*, 98–110.

4. Sundquist, *House Divided*, 131–59. See 148–51 for a discussion of Gavin. See also Michael Grimwood, "Faulkner and the Vocational Liabilities of Black Characterization," in *Faulkner and Race: Faulkner and Yoknapatawpha, 1986*, ed. Doreen Fowler and Ann J. Abadie

(Jackson: University Press of Mississippi, 1987), 255–71. Grimwood argues that Gavin's project and Ike's ledger reading are metaphors for Faulkner's misgivings about his own literacy and connects that to Faulkner's continuing perception of blacks as illiterate. His conclusion, that Faulkner was essentially disavowing his career, reduces the conflict too drastically and overlooks Faulkner's stubborn faith in his writing.

5. Richard Poirier, *A World Elsewhere: The Place of Style in American Literature* (New York: Oxford University Press, 1966), 78–83.

6. Darwin Turner discusses the entire Brownlee saga as it reveals Faulkner's own sympathy to the idea that freed slaves are worse off than those under the wing of a white master. Again the point is not to castigate Faulkner but to illustrate the impossibility of stepping completely outside our cultural assumptions. See his essay "Faulkner and Slavery" in Harrington and Abadie's *The South and Faulkner's Yoknapatawpha*, 76–77.

7. J. Douglas Canfield, "Faulkner's Grecian Urn and Ike McCaslin's Empty Legacies," *Arizona Quarterly* 36 (1980): 359–84.

8. See Sundquist's discussion of Ike's objections to Cass' interpretation of Keats, *House Divided*, 136–37. Sundquist notes that they center around Cass' omission of the line "yet, do not grieve" and connects that to Ike's central grief over the sins of his father.

9. In "The Two Wildernesses of 'The Bear' " (from *The Paradoxical Wilderness: Mailer and American Nature Writing*, [Ann Arbor, Mich.: University Microfilms, 1985], 71–111), Peter Pratt argues that Ike's desire to create a simple, absolute definition of the wilderness as the source of social values has allowed him to justify slavery. Pratt's reading offers a convincing explanation of the way that Ike's version of the wilderness—because it obliterates contradiction—paves the way for the Negro-as-noble-endurer image that echoes throughout Faulkner's characterizations of blacks.

10. See Sundquist, *House Divided*, 157–59, for an extended discussion of the connections between Ike's confrontation with the mulatto woman and white America's continuing guilt over miscegenation. He contends that the woman's question to Ike is the book's most powerful moment because it names the white race's problem: "Have you lived so long and forgotten so much that you don't remember anything you ever knew or felt or even heard about love?" (*Go Down, Moses*, 363).

11. For a provocative, Marxist reading of "The Bear" as Faulkner's bringing together the two cultures of the wilderness and the commissary, see Susan Willis, "Aesthetics of the Rural Slum: Contradictions and Dependency in 'The Bear,' " in *Faulkner: New Perspectives*, 174–94.

12. Sundquist notes that Gavin's project parallels the whole of Faulkner's career, *House Divided*, 151.

13. Blotner, *Faulkner* 2:1046, 1054.

14. Karl Zender gives a comprehensive discussion of Faulkner's social and financial responsibilities as they connect to his troubled sense of artistic power in the early 1940s. Zender sees *Go Down, Moses* as a parable for the artist's desire to recapture the ecstasy of writing; Zender also finds in Lucas Beauchamp, Faulkner's association of freedom with being black—another example of the pervasiveness of white assumptions in the novel. See *Crossing*, 66–83.

15. For the whole text of the song and discussion of its significance in the final section of the novel, see James Early, *The Making of "Go Down, Moses"* (Dallas: Southern Methodist University Press, 1972), 97–110.

16. Sundquist sees this as less about a woman than about mixing black and white blood, *House Divided*, 155. It is worth noting that Faulkner's obsession with blood lines in this book connects him to Gavin's theory of blood in *Light in August*.

17. Two of the best readings of Faulkner's language of myth are Sundquist's and Poirier's. In *House Divided*, 158–59, Sundquist presents a brilliant case for Faulkner's participation in white America's favorite myth of lost innocence, and Poirier, in *A World Elsewhere*, 78–84, was one of the first to argue that the language is an attempt to make Ike's experience transcendent and mythic.

5. The Language of Responsibility

1. Faulkner, "Address upon Receiving the Nobel Prize for Literature," in *The Portable Faulkner*, ed. Malcolm Cowley (New York: Viking Press, Penguin Books, 1978), 724. David Minter calls the Nobel address the "pinnacle from which [Faulkner] might be listened to by the young" in *William Faulkner: His Life and His Work* (Baltimore: Johns Hopkins University Press, 1980), 218.

2. In *Faulkner*, Blotner notes that Faulkner would go to São Paulo, site of the first writers' conference, only as a public service, 2:1503.

3. For more on Faulkner's increased sense of himself as a public figure, see Blotner, *Faulkner* 2:1479–1611 and Gary Stonum, *Faulkner's Career*, 157–59 and 195–201. Stonum discusses Faulkner's authority in terms of a growing sense of responsibility. Also, Karl Zender discusses the late novels, particularly *Requiem, Intruder*, and *A Fable* as they reveal a tension between warring impulses—on the one hand, to teach and to create art, and on the other, to revolt against teaching.

He sees these impulses as the compensation for loss that so haunts Faulkner. I would argue that they are equally issues of control. I think Faulkner's art is not founded just on his efforts to recapture a vanishing world but also on his (partial) recognition that his vision (of the premodern South) was always only partial. See *Crossing*, 130–43.

4. Meriwether and Millgate, eds., *Lion in the Garden*, 141.

5. See Gary Stonum's discussion of Faulkner's "last phase" as an elegy to his previous work, in *Faulkner's Career*, 153–94. See as well Zender (*Crossing*, 148–49), for discussion of Mink Snopes as the embodiment of Faulkner's desire to achieve immortality through art.

6. William Faulkner, *Knight's Gambit* (1949; reprint, New York: Random House, Vintage Books, 1978), 87. Subsequent references to this edition will appear parenthetically in the text.

7. See Blotner's account of Faulkner's comments as a panelist at "The Segregation Decision," at which he expressed doubts that "the Negro wants integration," *Faulkner* 2:1583.

8. William Faulkner, *The Town* (1957; reprint, New York: Random House, Vintage Books, 1961), 31. Subsequent references to this edition will appear parenthetically in the text.

9. William Faulkner, *Intruder in the Dust* (1948; reprint, New York: Random House, Vintage Books, 1972), 154–55. Subsequent references to this edition will appear parenthetically in the text.

10. Jehlen, *Class and Character*, 124–32.

11. Turner, "Faulkner and Slavery," 75. Also Karl Zender discusses Gavin's instruction of Chick in terms of Faulkner's own needs to believe in and protect the "illusion of a homogenous South." See *Crossing*, 126–30.

12. William Faulkner, *Requiem for a Nun* (1951; reprint, New York: Random House, Vintage Books, 1975), 80. Subsequent references to this edition will appear parenthetically in the text.

13. William Faulkner, *The Mansion* (1959; reprint, New York: Random House, Vintage Books, 1965), 392. Subsequent references to this edition will appear parenthetically in the text.

14. In the chapter, "Language in Paradise" from *Surprised by Sin*, Stanley Fish discusses the seventeenth-century belief that Adam's language established an accurate word-thing correlation and, if recovered, could bring humans to complete comprehension of the abstract. Naming was a first step that lent some control to the "dialectical investigation." Gavin partakes of this habit of mind, although not to the extent that he shuns metaphor or rhetoric as creating false appearances of reality. See Fish, *Surprised by Sin: The Reader in Paradise Lost* (New York: St. Martin's Press, 1967), 107–30.

15. See Stonum, *Faulkner's Career*, 188–89.

16. Karl Zender discusses the Gavin-Faulkner connection in terms

Works Cited

Abrams, M. H. *Natural Supernaturalism: Tradition and Revolution in Romantic Literature.* New York: W. W. Norton & Co., 1971.

Aiken, Conrad. "William Faulkner: The Novel as Form." In *Faulkner: A Collection of Critical Essays,* edited by Robert Penn Warren, 46–52. Englewood Cliffs, N.J.: Prentice-Hall, 1966.

Allen, William R. "The Imagist and Symbolist Views of the Function of Language: Addie and Darl Bundren in *As I Lay Dying.*" *Studies in American Fiction* 10 (Autumn 1982): 185–96.

Arnold, Matthew. "The Function of Criticism." In *Poetry and Criticism of Matthew Arnold,* edited by A. Dwight Culler, 237–58. Boston: Houghton Mifflin Co., Riverside, 1961.

Austin, J. L. *How To Do Things with Words.* Cambridge: Harvard University Press, 1962.

Bakhtin, Mikhail. "Discourse in the Novel." In *The Dialogic Imagination: Four Essays,* edited by Michael Holquist. Translated by Caryl Emerson and Michael Holquist, 259–422. Austin: University of Texas Press, 1981.

Beck, Warren. "William Faulkner's Style." In *Faulkner: A Collection of Critical Essays,* edited by Robert Penn Warren, 53–65. Englewood Cliffs, N.J.: Prentice-Hall, 1966.

Blake, Nancy. "Creation and Procreation: The Voice and the Name, or Biblical Intertextuality in *Absalom, Absalom!*" In *Intertextuality in Faulkner,* edited by Michel Gresset and Noel Polk, 128–43. Jackson: University Press of Mississippi, 1985.

Bleikasten, André. " 'Cet Affreux goût d'encre': Emma Bovary's Ghost in *Sanctuary.*" In *Intertextuality in Faulkner,* edited by Michel Gresset and Noel Polk, 36–56. Jackson: University Press of Mississippi, 1985.

———. "Fathers in Faulkner." In *The Fictional Father: Lacanian Readings of the Text,* edited by Robert Con Davis, 115–46. Amherst: University of Massachusetts Press, 1981.

173

————. *Faulkner's As I Lay Dying*, translated by Roger Little. Bloomington: Indiana University Press, 1973.

————. "For/Against an Ideological Reading of Faulkner's Novels." In *Faulkner and Idealism: Perspectives from Paris*, edited by Michel Gresset and Patrick Samway, S. J., 27–50. Jackson: University Press of Mississippi, 1983.

————. "In Praise of Helen." In *Faulkner and Women: Faulkner and Yoknapatawpha, 1985*, edited by Doreen Fowler and Ann J. Abadie, 128–143. Jackson: University Press of Mississippi, 1986.

————. *"Light in August:* The Closed Society and Its Subjects." In *New Essays on Light in August*, edited by Michael Millgate, 81–102. Cambridge: Cambridge University Press, 1987.

————. *The Most Splendid Failure: Faulkner's "The Sound and the Fury."* Bloomington: Indiana University Press, 1976.

————. "Of Sailboats and Kites: The 'Dying Fall' in Faulkner's *Sanctuary* and Beckett's *Murphy*." In *Intertextuality in Faulkner*, edited by Michel Gresset and Noel Polk, 57–72. Jackson: University Press of Mississippi, 1985.

Blotner, Joseph. *Faulkner: A Biography*. 2 vols. New York: Random House, 1974.

————. "William Faulkner's Essay on the Composition of *Sartoris*." *Yale University Library Gazette* 47 (Jan. 1973): 121–24.

Booth, Wayne C. "Freedom of Interpretation: Bakhtin and the Challenge of Feminist Criticism." In *Bakhtin: Essays and Dialogues on His Work*, edited by Gary Saul Morson, 145–76. Chicago: University of Chicago Press, 1986.

Brooks, Cleanth. Introduction. *Faulkner's Women: Characterization and Meaning*, by Sally R. Page, xi–xxii. Deland, Fla.: Everett/Edwards, 1972.

————. *William Faulkner: The Yoknapatawpha Country*. New Haven, Conn.: Yale University Press, 1963.

Broughton, Panthea R. *William Faulkner: The Abstract and the Actual*. Baton Rouge: Louisiana State University Press, 1974.

Burke, Kenneth. *Language as Symbolic Action*. Berkeley: University of California Press, 1966.

Canfield, J. Douglas. "Faulkner's Grecian Urn and Ike McCaslin's Empty Legacies." *Arizona Quarterly* 36 (1980): 359–84.

————, ed. *Twentieth Century Interpretations of Sanctuary*. Englewood Cliffs, N.J.: Prentice-Hall, 1982.

Chakovsky, Sergei. "Women in Faulkner's Novels: Author's Attitude and Artistic Function." In *Faulkner and Women: Faulkner and Yoknapatawpha, 1985*, edited by Doreen Fowler and Ann

J. Abadie, 41–57. Jackson: University Press of Mississippi, 1986.

Cowley, Malcolm. *The Faulkner-Cowley File: Letters and Memories, 1944–1964.* New York: Viking Press, 1966.

Cox, Dianne Luce. "A Measure of Innocence: *Sanctuary's* Temple Drake." *The Mississippi Quarterly* 39 (Summer 1986): 301–24.

D'Avanzo, Mario. "Bobbie Allen and the Ballad Tradition in *Light in August.*" *South Carolina Review* 8 (Nov. 1975): 22–29.

Diaz-Diocartez, Myriam. "Faulkner's Hen-House: Woman as Bounded Text." In *Faulkner and Women: Faulkner and Yoknapatawpha, 1985,* edited by Doreen Fowler and Ann J. Abadie, 235–69. Jackson: University Press of Mississippi, 1986.

Early, James. *The Making of "Go Down, Moses."* Dallas: Southern Methodist University Press, 1972.

Eliot, T. S. "The Love Song of J. Alfred Prufrock." In *The Collected Poems of T. S. Eliot, 1909–1962.* New York: Harcourt Brace & World, 1970.

Faulkner, William. *Absalom, Absalom!* 1936. Corrected text. New York: Random House, Vintage Books, 1987.

———. "Address Upon Receiving the Nobel Prize for Literature." In *The Portable Faulkner,* edited by Malcolm Cowley, 723–24. New York: Viking Press, Penguin Books, 1978.

———. *As I Lay Dying.* 1930. Corrected text. New York: Random House, Vintage Books, 1987.

———. *A Fable.* 1954. Reprint. New York: Random House, Vintage Books, 1978.

———. *Flags in the Dust.*New York: Random House, Vintage Books, 1973.

———. *Go Down, Moses.* 1940. Reprint. New York: Random House, Vintage Books, 1973.

———. *The Hamlet.* 1938. Reprint. New York: Random House, Vintage Books, 1956.

———. "An Introduction to *The Sound and the Fury.*" In *Faulkner: New Perspectives,* edited by Richard H. Brodhead, 21–28. Englewood Cliffs, N.J.: Prentice-Hall, 1983.

———. *Intruder in the Dust.* 1948. Reprint. New York: Random House, Vintage Books, 1972.

———. *Knight's Gambit.* 1949. Reprint. New York: Random House, Vintage Books, 1978.

———. *Light in August.* 1932. Corrected text. New York: Random House, Vintage Books, 1987.

———. *The Mansion.* 1959. Reprint. New York: Random House, Vintage Books, 1965.

————. *Mosquitoes*. 1927. Reprint. New York: Liveright, 1955.

————. *The Reivers: A Reminiscence*. New York: Random House, Vintage Books, 1962.

————. *Requiem for a Nun*. 1951. Reprint. New York: Random House, Vintage Books, 1975.

————. *Sanctuary*. 1931. Corrected text. New York: Random House, Vintage Books, 1987.

————. *Sanctuary: The Original Text*, edited by Noel Polk. 1931. Reprint. New York: Random House, 1981.

————. *Sartoris*. 1929. Reprint. New York: New American Library, Signet Classics, 1964.

————. *Selected Letters of William Faulkner*, edited by Joseph Blotner. New York: Random House, 1977.

————. *Soldier's Pay*. New York: Liveright, 1954.

————. *The Sound and the Fury*. 1929. Reprint. New York: Random House, Vintage Books, 1954.

————. "That Evening Sun." In *Collected Stories of William Faulkner*. New York: Random House, Vintage Books, 1977.

————. *The Town*. 1957. Reprint. New York: Random House, Vintage Books, 1961.

————. "Une Ballad des Femmes Perdues." *William Faulkner: Early Prose and Poetry*, edited by Carrel Collins, 54. Boston: Little, Brown and Co., 1962.

————. *The Unvanquished*. 1938. Reprint. New York: Random House, Vintage Books, 1965.

Fiedler, Leslie. *Love and Death in the American Novel*. New York: Stein and Day, 1975.

Fish, Stanley E. *Surprised by Sin: The Reader in Paradise Lost*. New York: St. Martin's Press, 1967.

Fowler, Doreen. "Joe Christmas and 'Womanshenegro.' " In *Faulkner and Women: Faulkner and Yoknapatawpha, 1985*, edited by Doreen Fowler and Ann J. Abadie, 144–61. Jackson: University Press of Mississippi, 1986.

Fowler, Doreen, and Ann J. Abadie, eds. *Faulkner and Women: Faulkner and Yoknapatawpha, 1985*. Jackson: University Press of Mississippi, 1986.

Frye, Northrop. *Anatomy of Criticism*. Princeton, N.J.: Princeton University Press, 1957.

Garrison, Joseph M., Jr. "Perception, Language, and Reality in *As I Lay Dying*." *Arizona Quarterly* 32 (1976): 16–30.

Gresset, Michel. "The 'Dying Fall' in *Sanctuary* and *Murphy*." In *Intertextuality in Faulkner*, edited by Michel Gresset and Noel Polk, 57–72. Jackson: University Press of Mississippi, 1985.

————. "The Space Between *Sanctuary*." In *Intertextuality in*

Faulkner, edited by Michel Gresset and Noel Polk. 16–35. Jackson: University Press of Mississippi, 1985.

Gresset, Michel, and Noel Polk, eds. *Intertextuality in Faulkner.* Jackson: University of Mississippi Press, 1985.

Grimwood, Michael. "Faulkner and the Vocational Liabilities of Black Characterization." In *Faulkner and Race: Faulkner and Yoknapatawpha, 1986*, edited by Doreen Fowler and Ann J. Abadie, 255–71. Jackson: University Press of Mississippi, 1987.

Grotjahn, Martin. "Beyond Laughter." In *Theories of Comedy*, edited by Paul Lauter, Jr., 523–29. New York: Doubleday & Co., 1964.

Guerard, Albert J. "Faulkner the Innovator." In *The Maker and the Myth*, edited by Evans Harrington and Ann J. Abadie, 71–88. Jackson: University Press of Mississippi, 1978.

———. "The Faulknerian Voice." In *The Maker and the Myth*, edited by Evans Harrington and Ann J. Abadie, 25–42. Jackson: University Press of Mississippi, 1978.

Guetti, James. *The Limits of Metaphor.* Ithaca, N.Y.: Cornell University Press, 1976.

Gwynn, Frederick, and Joseph Blotner, eds. *Faulkner in the University.* Charlottesville: University Press of Virginia, 1977.

Holquist, Michael. "Answering as Authoring: Mikhail Bakhtin's Trans-Linguistics." In *Bakhtin: Essays and Dialogues on His Work*, edited by Gary Saul Morson, 59–71. Chicago: University of Chicago Press, 1986.

Hunt, John W. "The Disappearance of Quentin Compson." In *Critical Essays on Walliam Faulkner: The Compson Family*, edited by Arthur F. Kinney, 366–80. Boston: G. K. Hall, 1982.

Hurd, Myles, "Faulkner's Horace: The Burden of Characterization and the Confusion of Meaning in *Sanctuary.*" *College Language Association Journal* 23 (June 1980): 416–30.

Irwin, John. *Doubling and Incest/Repetition and Revenge.* Baltimore: Johns Hopkins University Press, 1980.

Jehlen, Myra. *Class and Character in Faulkner's South.* New York: Columbia University Press, 1976.

Keiser, Merle Wallace. "*Flags in the Dust* and *Sartoris.*" In *Fifty Years of Yoknapatawpha*, edited by Doreen Fowler and Ann J. Abadie, 44–70. Jackson: University Press of Mississippi, 1980.

Kinney, Arthur F. *Faulkner's Narrative Poetics: Style as Vision.* Amherst: University of Massachusetts Press, 1978.

———. "*Sanctuary*: Style as Vision." In *Twentieth Century Interpretations of Sanctuary*, edited by J. Douglas Canfield, 109–19. Englewood Cliffs, N.J.: Prentice-Hall, 1982.

————, ed. *Critical Essays on William Faulkner: The Compson Family*. Boston: G. K. Hall, 1982.

Krause, David. "Reading Bon's Letter and Faulkner's *Absalom, Absalom!*" *PMLA* 99 (1984): 225–41.

————. "Reading Shreve's Letters and Faulkner's *Absalom, Absalom!*" *Studies in American Fiction* 11 (1983): 153–69.

Langford, Gerald. *Faulkner's Revision of "Sanctuary": A Collation of Unrevised Galleys and the Published Book*. Austin: University of Texas Press, 1972.

Langston, Beach. "The Meaning of Lena Grove and Gail Hightower in *Light in August*." *Boston University Studies in English* 5 (Spring 1961): 46–63.

Larsen, Eric. "The Barrier of Language: The Irony of Language in Faulkner." *Modern Fiction Studies* 12 (Spring 1967): 19–31.

Lilly, Paul R. "Caddy and Addie: Speakers of Faulkner's Impeccable Language." *Journal of Narrative Technique* 3 (Sept. 1973): 170–82.

Lind, Ilse DuSoir. "The Mutual Relevance of Faulkner Studies and Women's Studies: An Interdisciplinary Inquiry." In *Faulkner and Women: Faulkner and Yoknapatawpha, 1985*, edited by Doreen Fowler and Ann J. Abadie, 21–40. Jackson: University Press of Mississippi, 1986.

McDaniel, Linda E. "Horace Benbow: Faulkner's Endymion." *Mississippi Quarterly* 33 (Summer 1980): 363–70.

Matthews, John T. *The Play of Faulkner's Language*. Ithaca, N. Y.: Cornell University Press, 1982.

Meriwether, James, and Michael Millgate, eds. *Lion in the Garden*. Lincoln: University of Nebraska Press, 1968.

Millgate, Michael. "Faulkner's First Trilogy: *Sartoris, Sanctuary*, and *Requiem for a Nun*." In *Fifty Years of Yoknapatawpha*, edited by Doreen Fowler and Ann J. Abadie, 90–109. Jackson: University Press of Mississippi, 1980.

Minter, David. *William Faulkner: His Life and His Work*. Baltimore: Johns Hopkins University Press, 1980.

————, ed. *Twentieth Century Interpretations of Light in August*. Englewood Cliffs, N.J.: Prentice-Hall, 1969.

Mortimer, Gail L. *Faulkner's Rhetoric of Loss: A Study in Perception and Meaning*. Austin: University of Texas Press, 1983.

————. "Significant Absences: Faulkner's Rhetoric of Loss." *Novel* 14 (Spring 1981): 232–50.

————. "The Smooth, Suave Shape of Desire: Paradox in Faulknerian Imagery of Women." *Women's Studies* 13 (1986): 149–61.

O'Connor, William Van. "Rhetoric in Southern Writing: Faulkner." *The Georgia Review* 12 (Spring 1958): 83–86.

Page, Sally R. *Faulkner's Women: Characterization and Meaning.* Deland, Fla.: Everett/Edwards, 1972.

Parker, Robert. *William Faulkner and the Novelistic Imagination.* Champaign-Urbana: University of Illinois Press, 1985.

Peters, Erskine. *William Faulkner: The Yoknapatawpha World and Black Being.* Darby, Pa.: Norwood Editions, 1983.

Pierce, Constance. "Being, Knowing, and Saying in the 'Addie' Section of Faulkner's *As I Lay Dying.*" *Twentieth Century Literature* 26 (1980): 294–305.

Pitavy, François. *Faulkner's Light in August,* translated by Gillian E. Cook. Bloomington: Indiana University Press, 1973.

Poirier, Richard. *A World Elsewhere: The Place of Style in American Literature.* New York: Oxford University Press, 1966.

Polk, Noel. " 'The Dungeon Was Mother Herself': William Faulkner 1927–1931." In *New Directions in Faulkner Studies,* edited by Doreen Fowler and Ann J. Abadie, 61–93. Jackson: University Press of Mississippi, 1984.

———. "The Space Between *Sanctuary.*" In *Intertextuality in Faulkner,* edited by Michel Gresset and Noel Polk, 36–56. Jackson: University Press of Mississippi, 1985.

Pratt, Peter. "The Two Wildernesses of the 'The Bear.' " In *The Paradoxical Wilderness: Mailer and American Nature Writing,* by Peter Pratt, 71–111. Ann Arbor, Mich.: University Microfilms, 1985.

Riedel, F. C. "Faulkner as Stylist." *South Atlantic Quarterly* 56 (Autumn 1957): 462–79.

Ross, Stephen M. "The Evocation of Voice in *Absalom, Absalom!*" *Essays in Literature* 8 (1981): 135–49.

———. "The 'Loud World' of Quentin Compson."*Studies in the Novel* 7 (Summer 1975): 245–57.

———. "Oratory and the Dialogical in *Absalom, Absalom!*" In *Intertextuality in Faulkner,* edited by Michel Gresset and Noel Polk, 73–86. Jackson: University Press of Mississippi, 1985.

———. " 'Voice' in Narrative Texts: The Example of *As I Lay Dying.*" *PMLA* 94 (1979): 303–8.

Rossky, William. "*As I Lay Dying:* The Insane World." *Texas Studies in Literature and Language* 4 (Spring 1962): 87–95.

Slabey, Robert M. "Myth and Ritual in *Light in August.*" *Texas Studies in Literature and Language* 2 (Autumn 1960): 328–49.

Slatoff, Walter J. *Quest for Failure: A Study of William Faulkner.* Ithaca, N.Y.: Cornell University Press, 1960.

Stein, Jean. "William Faulkner." In *Writers at Work: The Paris Review,* edited by Malcolm Cowley, 122–41. New York: Viking Press, 1958.

Index

Judith Lockyer is an assistant professor of English at Albion College in Albion, Michigan. She teaches courses in American and women's literature and is currently at work on a study of narrative strategies in nineteenth-century African American women's fiction.